# THE PSYCHOLOGY OF CELEBRITY

Why are we fascinated by celebrities we've never met? What is the difference between fame and celebrity? How has social media enabled a new wave of celebrities?

*The Psychology of Celebrity* explores the origins of celebrity culture, the relationships celebrities have with their fans, how fame can affect celebrities, and what shapes our thinking about celebrities we admire. The book also addresses the way in which the media has been and continues to be an outlet for celebrities, culminating in the role of social media, reality television, and technology in our modern society.

Drawing on research featuring real-life celebrities from the Kardashians to Michael Jackson, *The Psychology of Celebrity* shows us that celebrity influence can have both positive and negative outcomes and the impact these can have on our lives.

**Gayle Stever** is an associate professor for SUNY/Empire State College, an institution that is focused on goals of lifelong learning, adult education, and access to higher education for all. She earned her Ph.D. in developmental psychology with an emphasis in the psychology of media from Arizona State University in 1994. She has spent the last 30 years studying fan/celebrity relationships from a participant observer perspective and to that end, has networked extensively into a number of fan groups of both pop stars like Michael Jackson, Madonna, or Josh Groban and also television stars like William Shatner, Rene Auberjonois or Alexander Siddig.

# THE PSYCHOLOGY OF EVERYTHING SERIES

The Psychology of Everything is a series of books that debunk the myths and pseudo-science surrounding some of life's biggest questions.

The series explores the hidden psychological factors that drive us, from our sub-conscious desires and aversions, to the innate social instincts handed to us across the generations. Accessible, informative, and always intriguing, each book is written by an expert in the field, examining how research-based knowledge compares with popular wisdom and illustrating the potential of psychology to enrich our understanding of humanity and modern life.

Applying a psychological lens to an array of topics and contemporary concerns – from sex to addiction to conspiracy theories – The Psychology of Everything will make you look at everything in a new way.

For further information about this series please visit
www.thepsychologyofeverything.co.uk.

# THE PSYCHOLOGY
# OF CELEBRITY

GAYLE STEVER

Routledge
Taylor & Francis Group

LONDON AND NEW YORK

First published 2019
by Routledge
2 Park Square, Milton Park, Abingdon, Oxon OX14 4RN

and by Routledge
711 Third Avenue, New York, NY 10017

Routledge is an imprint of the Taylor & Francis Group, an informa business

British Library Cataloguing-in-Publication Data
A catalogue record for this book is available from the British Library

Library of Congress Cataloging-in-Publication Data
A catalog record for this title has been requested

ISBN: 978-0-815-36955-4
ISBN: 978-0-815-36956-1
ISBN: 978-1-351-25210-2

Typeset in Joanna
by Apex CoVantage, LLC

# CONTENTS

# FOREWORD

Writing this book has been a journey for me. While I have developed expertise over the years on the subject of celebrities as they relate to their fans, the wider area of celebrity was newer to me. My journey began in 1988 with my master's thesis on Michael Jackson fans. In the intervening years, I have done further participant observer studies in the fandoms of *Star Trek: Deep Space Nine* and *Star Trek* in general, Madonna, Bruce Springsteen, Prince, George Michael, Paul McCartney, *Lord of the Rings*, and other media fandoms. I spent 2005 to the present on the fans of Josh Groban, who have been gracious, welcoming, and supportive. They have filled out hundreds of questionnaires, read drafts of papers, and helped in various other ways over the past 13 years. Josh Groban has read and made supportive remarks to me about various papers beginning back in 2006, the very first time I had the privilege of meeting him. My publications over the years are listed in the references at the back of this book and can be accessed at ResearchGate.net.

The purpose of this book is to give a window to the topic of celebrity through the lens of psychology, with an eye to making accessible the rather esoteric literature. This is a fancy way of saying that many other books are written at a postgraduate level, and, as such, are challenging reading. When I make recommendations for further reading throughout this book, I have tried to choose the most accessible sources and not recommend the more difficult ones. While this is a book for the student more than the scholar, I hope that some of the insights I have gained will be useful to any scholars who might happen onto this discussion.

Without the unfailing support of Empire State College/State University of New York and my colleagues there, this book would not have been possible. The college gave me release time to work on it, and my colleagues were interested and supportive throughout the process. I am very grateful for this.

Several of my actor/friends from *Deep Space Nine* have offered interviews and discussions for this book and those are Rene Auberjonois, Aron Eisenberg, Chase Masterson, Andrew Robinson, Armin Shimerman, and Alexander Siddig. The very presence of such kind and interested celebrities from such a prominent franchise as *Star Trek* and the depth with which they approached my questions makes a statement, in itself, about the nature of celebrity in today's culture. I am once again very grateful, as I have been in the past when these same people contributed in a major way to my writing and thinking about fan cultures.

I could not have completed this project without the support and insight of Eleanor Reedy, my editor. David Giles has been of enormous assistance along this writing journey, as were the initial blind reviewers of my proposal. Friends and colleagues Lorraine Lander and Jill Oliver have read, critiqued, and helped edit all of the chapters. Historian Wayne Willis gave me guidance on the project from start to finish, indeed, put me on to great examples of celebrity like Oscar Wilde, Walter Winchell, and Babe Ruth. Suzy Horton, Marie Freitas, Karen Santini, Linda Burnett, Marguerite Krause, Jan Learmonth, Gayle Lynne Gordon, and my sons, Scott and Paul Stever, have read chapters, given interviews, or provided invaluable feedback. My brothers, Jeff and Victor Yarter, have always encouraged and supported me in my work. Without my husband, John Stever's unfailing support (and critical proofreading eye), nothing I do would be possible.

Chapter 1 is an introduction to the study of celebrity with definitions and observations. Chapter 2 introduces a number of theories from social science, including psychology, that relate directly to the study of celebrity. Chapter 3 has examples taken from throughout history to show how fame and celebrity can be better understood. Chapter 4 is a discussion of how being famous affects the celebrity's life. Chapter 5 visits the relationship between celebrities and their fans. Chapter 6 includes the world of social media and the relatively recent development of the micro-celebrity but also deals with current 21st century trends in media.

# 1

## CELEBRITY
### An introduction

The last 20 years have seen an ever-increasing interest in celebrity, particularly by academic scholars. A brand new academic journal called *Celebrity Studies* debuted in 2010. On the inside cover of this journal it says, "*Celebrity Studies* is a journal that focuses on the critical exploration of celebrity, stardom, and fame. It seeks to make sense of celebrity by drawing upon a range of interdisciplinary approaches, media forms, historical periods, and national contexts." In the inaugural issue, Graeme Turner (2010) discussed why such a journal was needed and in this discussion, he explicates reasons that are very similar to why this book is needed, principally that celebrity has our attention and drives our consumption in a 21st-century media-dominated world.

Celebrity inhabits mediated space. Without conversations about celebrities (some would call it "gossip"), there is no fame or celebrity, and without a medium within which to hold the conversations, celebrity simply does not exist. Celebrity is a social thing. It does not exist in isolation.

## DEFINING CELEBRITY

A great deal has been written about celebrity, particularly in the most recent 20 years (which at this writing is 1998 to 2018), but it is still difficult to lock down a succinct definition of celebrity.

The notion of celebrity isn't simply being known or "famous," but rather why a person is known. Karen Sternheimer (2015) defines celebrity as "anyone who is watched, noticed and known by a critical mass of strangers" (p. 2). Celebrity is delineated as an interest in the person's personal life.

## CELEBRITY: STATE VS. TRAIT

In most writings about celebrity, the word is used as a noun. A person is a celebrity. But what if we thought of celebrity, not as a noun, but rather as a characteristic of an individual, an adjective? We could then talk about celebrity in the same way other characteristics of individuals are discussed. There is a common thread in personality research that tries to differentiate states vs. traits. For example, is extroversion a trait of an individual, as in "Joe is an extrovert?" Or is it a state as in "Helen is in an extroverted mood today?"

Using the word "celebrity" in this way, we could talk about a person's celebrity as being a state that is potentially transient. Rather than a person being a celebrity, a person can be in a state of celebrity, or could potentially possess the trait of celebrity. Brad Pitt is a celebrity, and that is liable to be a constant trait for him as he has been famous for a very long time. But some individuals are in a state of celebrity that may be here today and gone tomorrow, although transient celebrity is something that most often exists only at the lower levels of the celebrity hierarchy, e.g., single events such as those that happen with a rescue or other single heroic act (van de Rijt, Shor, Ward, & Skiena, 2013).

## CELEBRITIES ARE THOSE WHO DRAW OUR ATTENTION

Van Krieken (2012) has suggested that in our complex society, attention is a scarce resource. There are so many things to draw our attention, that where we invest it has to be selective. Celebrities are those who, through unique characteristics or accomplishments or behaviors, draw our attention. When the individual has succeeded in drawing our attention, we could say that the person is in a state of celebrity, or is being celebrated, either for accomplishments or for other unique and attention-drawing characteristics. Sometimes attention is drawn for simply having certain characteristics as in the case of Oscar Wilde, who in the 19th century set out to gain attention by being as outrageous as possible. Wilde achieved a state of celebrity long before he had really accomplished anything that was worthy of fame. For a famous person (achieved celebrity), the attention comes after something has been accomplished, but for those individuals for whom attention is the goal, sometimes nothing whatsoever really has been accomplished but rather the person has used various means to draw attention. This is celebrity without fame, fame being distinguished as being known for a noteworthy accomplishment of some kind. The Kardashians are the most often cited example of attention seekers who have not accomplished much, but they are far from the only ones doing this.

More often a person becomes a celebrity after having achieved fame such as the case of Charles Lindbergh where he became a celebrity after achieving the first transatlantic flight, but Oscar Wilde is an example of someone who achieved celebrity and then after he was already well known, wrote books and plays for which he is known today. Would his plays have been noticed had he not been known? This is a difficult question, one that is not easy to answer, but it is easy to speculate that they might not have been.

## FAME AND CELEBRITY: THE SAME OR DIFFERENT?

One important distinction in some of the writings on this subject is the difference between celebrity and fame. It might seem like a simple thing to say, "Celebrities are people who are famous," but upon careful analysis, that isn't such a simple thing to say after all. Let's consider why.

Rojek (2001) is identified in multiple sources (e.g., Luckhurst & Moody, 2005) as first making clear the distinctions among ascribed, achieved, and attributed celebrity. The first is fame by virtue of birth, the second by virtue of renown or accomplishment, and attributed celebrity is that situation where a person is "known for well-knownness" (Boorstin, 1961, p. 57).

Turner (2004) concurred with a distinction between celebrity and other forms of renown: "We can map the precise moment a public figure becomes a celebrity. It occurs at the point at which media interest in their activities is transferred from reporting on their public role . . . to investigating the detail of their private lives" (p. 8).

Giles (2000) has developed a taxonomy of fame, in which he described four types of fame: public figures (roles such as political or public service roles), fame based on merit (fame through enduring achievement), show-business stars (singers, actors, etc.), and accidental fame (such as fame through association or through being in the right place at the right time). He then enumerated levels of fame from domain specific (within a particular group), to fame in the local community, to national, and then international fame. He conducted a study with 160 undergraduate students that showed the robustness of his model, with most celebrities fitting easily into the levels and categories proposed.

Driessens (2013) pointed out the confusing use of terms and the disagreement among scholars about meanings, and that each scholar who has written about celebrity has stressed different meanings. For example, Dyer (2004) and also Marshall (1997) have focused on celebrity as a commodity, while Couldry (2003) focused more on celebrity as a creation of media. Among many writers there appears to be a disagreement as to whether or not new forms of celebrity make it more democratic or rather just create new status hierarchies.

Some of the vocabulary used in the study of celebrity can be challenging. For example, let's take the words "celebritization" and "celebrification." Driessens (2013) pointed out that these words are confused through much of the writings on celebrity (Gamson, 1994; Turner, 2004), and determining what each term means and how it differs from the other takes some explanation. According to Driessens, "celebritization" happens when a field of study or cause draws on prominent people in order to bring that cause or area to public attention. When environmental activists concerned with global warming used the celebrity of figures like Al Gore, Leonardo di Caprio, or Mark Ruffalo to promote their cause, that field was said to be celebritized (Boykoff & Goodman, 2009). "Celebrification" happens when an ordinary individual becomes a celebrity. One other way to look at these two terms is to note that celebrification happens to an individual, whereas celebritization happens to a group.

One of the struggles when writing about celebrity and fame is to try to keep the terms distinct when, in fact, they really are a part of one another. Many writers use the terms interchangeably. In this discussion I will try to maintain the distinction between fame as achieved celebrity as opposed to celebrity as ascribed or attributed. If this isn't clear to you, that's OK. It isn't always clear to everyone else either! But here is an example to help.

## AN EXAMPLE OF FAME VS. CELEBRITY

To recap, in order to have a celebrity, you must have an audience or public, because one is defined in relation to the other. The words "fame," "renown," or even "achieved celebrity" are used to talk about a person who is well known for an outstanding accomplishment. "Celebrity" is reserved for knowing about a person's personal life and behavior apart from the initial action that brought them to our attention. A person can be both famous and a celebrity, or one or the other (or neither).

The example I found that made this most clear to me was an article written by Trevor Parry-Giles (2008) on the subject of United States President John Adams. Parry-Giles takes David McCullough (2002) to task for his biography on Adams, alleging that he "promotes this founder's celebrity rather than his meritorious fame" (p. 83). According to this historian, one can look at Adams in terms of the things he accomplished, the things for which he is best known, his presidency, his part in the Declaration of Independence, his foreign diplomacy, political philosophy, and other accomplishments central to the history of the country. But instead McCullough champions Adams on a personal level, relying on the "affective rhetorics of praise and admiration that dominate contemporary celebrity politics" (p. 88). To state that Adams contributed in a major way to the drafting of the Declaration of Independence is to focus on a thing for which he is famous. But to say that Adams was a great guy, a good husband, a passionate defender of the country, and an all-around good person is to focus on his person rather than on his accomplishments. This would appear to be what differentiates celebrity from fame.

## IS CELEBRITY A STRICTLY MODERN PHENOMENON OR HAS IT EXISTED IN COMPLEX SOCIETIES THROUGHOUT HISTORY?

A number of scholarly books have been written that focus on the history of celebrity including those by Braudy (1997, Inglis (2010), and Cashmore (2014). In each of these discussions, some overall themes emerge with respect to how to divide human history into distinct eras of celebrity.

Some writers believe that celebrity was a 20th-century invention (e.g., Schickel, 2000), but many others feel that the celebrity dates back to Alexander, The Great (Braudy, 1997) or the Caesars (Garland, 2010), in other words to 60 BC or even earlier.

Others argue that celebrity as we know it today emerged in 1660 with actors achieving star status in the theater in London (Luckhurst & Moody, 2005), and also later on Broadway in New York City (Gabler, 1995). With the rise of visual media, including photographs, the era of "the image" was born (Boorstin, 1961), with the advent of silent films in 1902 bringing image fame to a much higher level. Stars like Greta Garbo and Charlie Chaplin became instantly recognizable in this era.

## 20TH-CENTURY CELEBRITY

Also prevalent in the early 20th century were popular radio broadcasts and the stars who were featured on them. The "talkies" (films with sound) began an era of major film stars who were promoted by large studios like MGM (Gardner, 1990). Television begins another distinct era, with celebrities entering the intimacy of our living rooms and making us feel "at home" with them (Horton & Wohl, 1956). "In 1945, there were probably fewer than 10,000 sets in the country. This figure soared to about 6 million in 1950, and to almost 60 million by 1960" (The World Book Encyclopedia. Chicago: World Book Inc., 2003: 119). In the 1980s, a shift away from mass media and towards specialized media markets meant there were many more celebrities, but it became harder and harder for an individual celebrity to captivate the entire marketplace.

## THE CULTURE OF CELEBRITY

Almost one century ago, a novel system of social status emerged in human history. From its beginnings on the coasts of North America, it grew into a global hierarchy, entwining itself into huge spheres of the social world. By the late 20th century, members of the high-status group had come to expect obsequious deference, exact significant financial tribute, and lay claim to legal privilege, as aristocratic and caste elites did in earlier centuries. But the new status system was different. It was born out of capitalism and mass media, and its dynamics reflected the conditions of the modern era. This system is called celebrity.

(Kurzman et al., 2007, p. 347)

There are a number of points to be made about this paragraph that make it worth quoting in its entirety. First of all, it highlights an aspect of one disagreement amongst scholars as to when "celebrity" began. Individuals who meet the definition of celebrity go back at least as far as Alexander, the Great. Garland (2010) framed his discussion of celebrity using examples from ancient history and emphatically maintained that "the phenomenon of celebrity culture is by no means peculiar to our age" (p. 484). In creating his argument, he enumerated specific psychological factors contributing to the creation of celebrity that have existed throughout recorded human history. These included the desire for recognition, the desire to be remembered, the desire for wealth, sex, and power, and in many cases, an altruistic motive to promote causes that the celebrity believed to be important. He applied all of these factors to the case of Emperor Augustus in ancient Rome.

But "celebrity society," (Van Krieken, 2012) a culture dominated by the status hierarchy that is determined specifically by being a member of an elite class of people who are well known and talked about, dates back to the early 20th century. While celebrities certainly were identified in the 1700s and 1800s (Brock, 2006; Luckhurst & Moody, 2005), the dominance of celebrity culture as the defining aspect of status in society is a much more recent development.

What emerged in the 20th century was celebrity-driven culture and not the concept of celebrity. Celebrities had been around for a long time, but the focus on celebrity as a driving cultural and economic force was perpetuated by mass media, in particular visual mass media, which originated and proliferated mostly in the 20th century with the introduction of film, television, and ultimately the Internet.

Previous incarnations of celebrity were spawned from the photograph, the monument, the printed word, and other "slower" forms of media. An example of this was Abraham Lincoln, the first president to be recognized for his face because of widely circulated photos (Braudy, 1997). The greater speed with which fame could be achieved and communicated with the advent of moving pictures was what made the 20th-century phenomenon different.

The era of mass media began with industrialization (Toffler, 1980) so it might make sense to draw a connection between the industrialized beginnings of mass media and celebrity. The invention of the printing press formally marks, at the very least, the potential for mass media and that was about 1440. Luckhurst and Moody (2005) traced the derivation of critical terms, noting that the term "fame" was used as early as 1290 and that "famous" gained recognized usage in the Shakespearean era. Celebrate, celebrity, and celebrated all first appeared around the 1600s. They differentiated the term "notoriety" as being associated with being known as the result of controversy and scandal.

Driessens (2013) pointed out that "little attention has been paid to the prevalence of celebrity in previous epochs" (p. 644) and took exception to Schickel's (2000) assertion that celebrity is a 20th-century phenomenon. Graeme Turner (2004) asserted, Braudy "is one of the . . . few to have addressed contemporary celebrity . . . by insisting on its continuity with earlier versions of fame" (p. 9), given that others position modern celebrity as fundamentally a phenomenon of the mass media (Rojek, 2001). Those who agree with him include Barry (2008), Gledhill (1991), Sternheimer (2015), Mole (2009), as well as Luckhurst and Moody (2005). Perhaps the problem was the lack of distinction made between individual celebrities who are common in early history, as opposed to the celebrity society described by Van Krieken (2012).

## CELEBRITY AND THE RISE OF INDUSTRIAL SOCIETY

All of the preceding discussion is related to Alvin Toffler's (1990) theory about power shifts (covered more thoroughly in Chapter 2). He explains that at the beginning of human history, power was determined by physical strength. With the shift to industrial society, power also shifted to a society based on material wealth. During the third wave of change, which he identified as being roughly in the 1970s and 1980s (Toffler, 1980), power shifts once again from physical might, to wealth to a third arena – information. Recall that we have said that "celebrity" is determined by the allocation of a limited resource called "attention." These are two ways of saying a similar thing as status conferred by those who command our attention, and power based on information are two sides of the same angle.

The individual celebrity has been around for many centuries, but a social structure that glorifies renown has happened mostly with the advent of mass visual media. Many famous people were launched into a life of fame through the printing of books, plays, newspapers, and other forms of the printed word; however, it was the movies that ushered in the era of the celebrity as a recognizable face. Certainly, photographs were a precursor to moving pictures, but the ability to relate on a human level to the intimate stranger is multiplied by the moving and talking image.

There have been vocal critics of celebrity society. Neil Postman (2006), in his book *Amusing Ourselves to Death: Discourse in the Age of Show Business*, warned of the dangers of a society driven by images rather than ideas. Jerry Mander in 1978 made a similar cautionary argument in his book *Four Arguments for the Elimination of Television*. By revering people for form rather than substance, by electing officials because of their pleasing images and articulate speech rather than for their grasp of ideas and knowledge of how to solve problems, society was heading down a path of self-destruction according to these authors.

After moving away from the class system of England to form a new nation without aristocracy and royalty, 200 years later, the United States had succeeded in recreating its own form of aristocracy and class system. That idea is at the heart of Kurzman (2007) and also the writings of Daniel J. Boorstin (1961) who cautioned that famous people were no longer heroic but instead were simply known for being well known. This is at the heart of the argument that celebrity is a shadow of true fame, based on being talked about rather than having actually done something worthy of note.

## ADDITIONAL HISTORICAL PERSPECTIVES

To understand how our current system of celebrity evolved, I recommend *The Power Elite* by Mills (1981). He described in some detail the way "society" (an elite group of upper class individuals recognized as being part of "important" people of the day) evolved into celebrity society, this happening at the end of the 19th century and the beginning of the 20th. He defined celebrities as "The Names that need no further identification" (p. 72). While "society" existed in the parlors and homes of the elite, celebrity society existed in public places and was referred to as "cafe society." It took generations to break into society, but cafe society's borders were more permeable, and enough money and notoriety were all that was needed to become a participant. The term "cafe society" was coined in 1919 by Maury Paul specifically to describe people who socialized together in public but weren't personal friends who visited one another at home (Van Krieken, 2012). The important point for our discussion here is to understand that the transition from private aristocracy to public celebrity was a gradual one that took place over a period of decades and was a social transition much facilitated by the increasing dominance of mass media in partnership with institutions like the theater, instrumental at that time in the creation of celebrity for a number of individuals.

As noted by Van Krieken (2012), one of the early people to capitalize on mass media and 20th-century forms of media was Walter Winchell. He was prominent in various forms of media in the early 20th century, beginning with a gossip column in a newspaper that eventually became nationally syndicated. Winchell moved on to radio and even starred in movies, eventually acknowledged by the 1930s as one of the most powerful people in celebrity society. Winchell used celebrity gossip as a primary form of media influence and celebrities sought to have themselves inserted into his columns in order to gain more publicity for themselves. It is possible to recognize the beginnings of what came to be known as "tabloid journalism" in Winchell's columns (Gabler, 1995).

Then in the 1950s, the invention of television was to change celebrity culture forever. Horton and Wohl (1956) discuss the importance of the presence of personalities in the privacy of our homes in developing what they called "parasocial interaction," or intimacy and interaction at a distance with those who do not reciprocate (Stever, 2016b).

James Bennett (2011) has discussed in depth the difference between television personalities, television stars, and other forms of stars and celebrities. He argues that television personalities have a unique place in celebrity culture. While it is easy to argue that television personalities are in the category of people well known for being well known, Bennett argued that doing this kind of work requires a special kind of televisual (and in some cases vocational) skill. Television personalities are presenters on television who appear as themselves and host a variety of kinds of programs, from game shows and talk shows to cooking shows and do-it-yourself presentations. Newscasters fall into this category as well. All of the early work in parasocial interaction focused on these kinds of celebrities. A big distinction is that these people play themselves on television as opposed to a fictional character. But as Horton and Wohl (1956) pointed out, television brings these people into the intimacy of one's home in a way that other kinds of earlier celebrities were not.

By the 1980s, television had evolved from four basic networks (CBS, PBS, NBC, and ABC) to a multitude of cable channels. This coincided with the beginnings of Toffler's third wave of change (discussed at length in Chapter 2). Personal computers became prevalent also in the 1980s after the first Commodore computer was offered in 1977, but initially they were disk drive machines that did not support Internet. It was in 1995 that the Internet became more widely available with the advent of Windows 95. Starting with just 0.4% of the world (16 million users) having access, by 2017 almost half of the world (over 4 billion users) had access to the Internet (www.internetworldstats.com/emarketing.htm; (https://smallbiztrends.com/2013/05/the-complete-history-of-social-media-infographic.html).

Ellis Cashmore (2014) has made the argument that beginning in the 1980s, following the success of Madonna, it was no longer necessary to avoid scandal or to try to keep up a positive image to have success as a celebrity. The attention Madonna received from being controversial opened up an entire new way of thinking. In addition, Madonna was one of the artists whose fans I interviewed on the 1990 *Blonde Ambition* tour, and the prevailing theme of those interviews was that Madonna was someone to be admired for the way she had taken charge of her own career in a social system that objectified and controlled women. In fact, the burgeoning women's movement in the 1980s set the stage for someone like Madonna to have this kind of success.

The next big media change that affected the history of celebrity is the introduction of social media to the Internet. Earliest forms of social media included a website called "Six Degrees" which in 1997 allowed users to create profiles and link to other users. The first blogging websites originated in 1999, a form of social media that is still popular today. LinkedIn and MySpace were created in the early 2000s, followed by YouTube in 2005, Twitter and Facebook in 2007, and specialized social media websites, for example Tumblr, Spotify, Foursquare, and Pinterest, in the years just after. By 2017, Facebook had over 1.9 billion users, while other social media followed far behind with Instagram having about 400 million, Twitter about 320 million, and Google about 300 million.

## THE VARIOUS ACADEMIC DISCIPLINES ON CELEBRITY

Most of what has been written has not (with a few notable exceptions) been written by psychologists, but more frequently by sociologists, cultural studies scholars, humanities (including film) scholars, economists, and historians.

Dictionary.com defines psychology as "the science of the mind or of mental states and processes; the science of human and animal behavior." By contrast, sociology, another discipline that deals often with the concepts of fame and celebrity, is defined as "the science or study of the origin, development, organization, and functioning of human society; the science of the fundamental laws of social relationship, institutions, etc."

Cultural studies, defined variously as either a sub-discipline of communication or as inter-disciplinary, has Turner's (2004, 2014) *Understanding Celebrity*. Sociologists have the already mentioned Sternheimer's *Celebrity Culture and the American Dream* (2015) and also Ferris and Harris (2011) *Stargazing: Celebrity, Fame and Social Interaction*, as well as Rojek's (2001) *Celebrity*. The humanities and specifically film studies offer books like Holmes and Redmond's (2006) *Framing Celebrity: New Directions in Celebrity Culture*. The most important psychology book on celebrity is David Giles' *Illusions of Immortality* (2000).

The emphasis in this book will be on celebrity as it relates to the mind, mental states and processes, and the behavior of the individual, both alone or in groups. Sociology has said important things about celebrity's effect on society. Economists have discussed how the economy is influenced by the culture of celebrity. Cultural studies scholars have focused on the "star" system and its effect on visual media. We'll touch on those things, but in this book we want to be psychologists and understand how celebrity affects the individual, both the celebrity and audience member.

Now in Chapter 2, we move to theories in social science, including psychology, that are important to the study of celebrity.

# 2

## PSYCHOLOGY AND CELEBRITY
### Social science theories

This chapter is a summary of key theories in psychology and related social sciences that are foundational to our discussion of celebrity. Each of these theories supports the study of celebrity and explains key aspects of our societal and individual fascination with celebrities and the famous. At the end of the chapter, an application of one of the theories illustrates how theory can apply directly to real-life practice.

Theories are important in order to organize our thinking and help tie together related concepts. Each of these theories has recommendations for further reading at the back of the book. Look there for specific references and additional information for each theory.

## ALBERT BANDURA, SOCIAL LEARNING THEORY, AND SOCIAL COGNITIVE THEORY

Albert Bandura was a mid-20th-century psychologist who was one of the first to question key principles of behaviorism, a paradigm that had dominated psychology from 1913 to the 1960s. A key premise of behaviorism had been that learning takes place through reinforcement and that without it, learning doesn't happen. Bandura recognized that learning can take place by watching other people receive reinforcements and punishments, and he conducted a famous experiment where children watched an adult play with a Bobo doll (a large inflatable doll that when knocked over would pop back up). Children who saw an adult model play violently with the Bobo doll played with it the same way, where children who saw more normal play with the Bobo doll played with it without the violent acting out of the other group. Bandura called this vicarious learning (www.youtube.com/watch?v=dmBqwWlJg8U).

In 2001, Bandura wrote an essay about mass communication and his social cognitive theory. In it he proposed that social cognitive theory provides a conceptual framework for understanding how media influence changes human behavior. He described his concept of reciprocal determinism, which challenged the more linear thinking of behaviorists who had described learning as "stimulus-response-reinforcement." In that theory, a stimulus causes a reaction, and the reaction has neither a positive nor a negative outcome for the actor (for more information see McLeod, 2015). Bandura's model recognized that any behavior is influenced not just by one stimulus but by many stimuli. This system includes personal factors such as "cognitive, affective, and biological events, behavioral patterns, and environmental events" (p. 266), and these factors each influence the others in both directions. So, for example, when someone reacts to the behavior of another, the reaction changes both people and it also can change the environment within which they both live. If my friend gets angry with me, and I react with anger, we each are affected by the other's behavior and our environment becomes more tense as a result. Simple "stimulus-response-reinforcement" doesn't capture that.

Vicarious learning and reciprocal determinism are very important in an environment saturated by media, where people known through media become role models for their viewers, and the viewers in turn shape the behavior of the media personalities by their actions. A famous athlete endorses a product, and her fans run right out and buy that product; that sends a message to both the athlete and the company producing the product that encourages them to pair up for future endorsements. Related to this idea is the concept of "branding," which says that by adopting a persona in relationship to marketed items, those items become associated with the endorser. Chapter 6 on social media will talk further about this concept of "branding."

## ERIK ERIKSON AND LIFESPAN DEVELOPMENT THEORY

Erik Erikson was the first developmental psychologist to suggest that development is a lifelong process that continues into adulthood. Other developmental theories had focused on infancy, childhood, and adolescence, recognizing that each stage of development had unique aspects and defining characteristics. For Erikson, each stage was associated with a crisis and the task of the developing individual was to overcome the crisis of each stage. While the tasks of the earlier years built on developmental theories that were already in existence, his idea that adulthood had stages and tasks was a new idea, one that was later expanded by Daniel J. Levinson. Erikson's theory is important to the study of celebrities and their fans because the motivations to become a big fan of someone are related to the tasks of the life stage the individual is in. For example, adolescence has the task of identity development, and it is during this stage that people are more likely to seek out celebrity role models with whom to identify.

The development of identity is a common topic in the various articles and books about celebrity. When Erikson wrote about identification or identity development beginning back in the 1950s, he was talking about the way that humans develop an answer to the "Who am I?" question that we all begin to ask ourselves as we go through adolescence. While our personal heroes and models are most often parents and family members, we typically do not want to look and dress like or listen to the same music as our parents. It is in this way that celebrities can specifically have power over the younger generation.

As a result of identification with and aspiration to various types of celebrity, reality television has exploded in the early 21st century from four such programs in the year 2000 to 320 programs by the year 2015 (Yahr, Moore, & Chow, 2015). These programs are particularly popular with adolescents, which Erikson's theory of identity development would have predicted. In the area of advertising, research has shown that celebrity spokespersons are far more effective if identification is at work (Basil, 1996).

In a study on Elvis Presley fans as well as Elvis impersonators (Fraser & Brown, 2002), it was found that they had a strong identification with Elvis as a role model and he had influenced their lifestyle and values in a significant way. In my own dissertation research (Stever, 1994, 2009), identification was one of the biggest factors recognized in documents where fans had described the reasons why their favorite celebrity was such an important part of their lives. Soukup (2006) found that identification with a celebrity was a prominent factor in a fan's decision to participate on that celebrity's website. Overall, it is clear that in the search for "Who am I?" by adolescents in particular, identification with a favorite celebrity can be a key factor in that struggle.

Early adulthood is a stage where the task is intimacy, and people begin to figure out whom they want to be with, after having figured out who they are. Because girls are so often encouraged to relate their identity to the person they are with, Erikson talked about how sometimes girls work on intimacy before they get to identity. In my doctoral dissertation, I discussed this phenomenon, having noted that teenage girls were more likely to identify "crushes" as primary in their fan interests while teenage boys were more likely to talk about celebrities with whom they had identified or saw as role models. Of note was the fact that in their 20s, this emphasis reversed with more men relating romantic attraction to a favorite celebrity and more women relating that their favorite celebrity was a role model for them (regardless of whether the target celebrity was a man or a woman).

In middle adulthood, where the task is generativity (giving back to the next generation after having been nurtured by the previous generation), fan interest was very often driven by shared philanthropic activity with a favorite celebrity. While some (Putnam,

2001) have suggested that the current generation of adults is less active in philanthropic activity than previous generations, it may be that there has been a shift from local traditional charitable activity to a less location focused kind of effort. Less involvement in local civic organizations has been countered by activism coming from new places and new networks not grounded in physical location. Rather, they are brought together through networks that involve various kinds of media. For middle adults, this opportunity for generativity through new media is an important development, with celebrity role models often the source of motivation for this activity.

In my own fieldwork in fan studies, every fan group with whom I networked had significant charity work as a part of the activity of the group. For the fan clubs of *Star Trek: Deep Space Nine*, in collaboration with the actors on the show, this meant raising upwards of $350,000 for the actors' charities during the period from 1994 to 2003. Groban-ites for Charity, a fan organized arm of the Josh Groban foundation, raised well over a million dollars for his foundation in the years from 2003 to 2010. Charity work in organized fandom has been the rule and not the exception.

## ATTACHMENT THEORY

Beginning in the 1960s, John Bowlby and Mary Ainsworth devel-oped a theory of attachment that recognized that infants seek prox-imity to their caregivers in order to feel safe and secure. Each has an inborn repertoire of behaviors. Caregivers who connect with infants in healthy ways promote secure bonds. The attachment system is a delicate balance between both proximity seeking and exploratory behaviors with the purpose of keeping the baby safe but also pro-moting growth and discovery.

Phillip Shaver and Cindy Hazan (1994) learned through their work that this same proximity seeking to facilitate security and a sense of safety was present in adult romantic relationships. The difference was that adult partners take turns being the caregiver, and the sense of security in this case is mutual. In both infancy and adulthood, balanced relationships that facilitate both proximity and exploration were the hallmarks of secure attachment.

In my own work, I noticed fans who obtained a sense of felt security and safe haven from the presence of their favorite celebrities and those celebrities' works in their own lives (Stever, 2011c, 2013). Remember that the word "parasocial" means non-reciprocal (see Chapter 1), so a parasocial relationship is when we know people in media who don't and usually can't know us back. The idea of a parasocial attachment, this sense of comfort provided by the fan/celebrity relationship, is an example of an attachment not reciprocated with any response from the media figure.

## ERVING GOFFMAN AND THE DRAMATURGICAL PERSPECTIVE

> All the world's a stage,
> And all the men and women merely players;
> They have their exits and their entrances,
> And one man in his time plays many parts.
>
> As You Like It by William Shakespeare (Act II Scene VII)

> It is no mere historical accident that the word person, in its first meaning, is a mask. It is rather a recognition of the fact that everyone is always and everywhere, more or less consciously, playing a role. . . . It is in these roles that we know each other; it is in these roles that we know ourselves.
>
> – Robert Ezra Park, Race and Culture, 1950, p. 249

Goffman suggested, in his 1959 book, that the goal of behavior is to control, as much as possible, the conduct of others. His theory is referred to as the dramaturgical approach to person perception, the idea that all of human behavior is "performed" in a manner not unlike Shakespeare's allegation, put forth above, that we are all players on the stage of life.

Applying Goffman, it makes sense to suppose that by achieving fame or celebrity, an individual has widened the circle of people whose behavior can be controlled. If that behavior involves spending money, the celebrity can increase her or his own material wealth by influencing others to spend it on items that will cause the celebrity to profit. By achieving celebrity, one has the potential to influence others to buy books, music, movie tickets, or a host of other things that would bring profit to that celebrity. This is what is meant when we say celebrity drives capitalism and why the phrase "rich and famous" is recognized intuitively as a likely pairing of terms.

We work hard to control the impression we make on others. It is important to realize that everyone does this, not just celebrities. Imparting some sort of nefarious agenda towards the famous person for only showing his or her best side is a failure to recognize that to do otherwise would be abnormal in the extreme. We all play parts in life, and we want others to see these parts as authentic and genuine. Thus, the celebrity "performance" is not terribly dissimilar to the everyday performances of all people everywhere.

Another of Goffman's ideas is that all of personal reality is on a continuum between sincerity and cynicism. You present yourself and either believe in that presentation (sincerity) or know you are playing a part (cynicism). Most of us are nearer the middle on this scale, presenting a self that we hope is mostly true but knowing that sometimes we are putting on our "game face." I observed this at the end of my mother's life, when she was failing, but would act as if everything were fine, and sometimes even convinced herself that this was true.

So, the allegation put forth that celebrities aren't showing their true selves is one that should be taken with this understanding, that they are doing what we all do, but just for a wider audience. Given how much of the current literature on social media in particular talks about "back stage" and "performance," a good grasp of Goffman is critical to understanding celebrities and their place in our culture.

## HENRI TAJFEL AND SOCIAL IDENTITY THEORY

Henri Tajfel (1970), a social psychologist from Poland, developed "social identity theory," which addressed the origins of prejudice and stereotyping, explaining why people see themselves as members of various ingroups, resulting in corresponding outgroups. His research established the homogeneity of the outgroup, the idea that individuals tend to see the members of groups of which they are not a member as being "all alike" while they see the groups within which they are members as varied and diverse. To apply that, as a woman, I might think that women are a varied group of unique individuals who are as much different as they might, by virtue of their gender, be alike; conversely, "those men are all alike."

This tendency to ascribe homogeneity to the outgroup has been the source of much of the tendency for academics to see celebrities as "all the same" in many key aspects. Tajfel also felt that personal interaction with the outgroup is the key to breaking down stereotypes, but herein is a big problem. Personal interaction with celebrities is either seen as too difficult to achieve by many scholars or perhaps is seen as not worth the trouble. Thus, academics miss the opportunity to see the uniqueness in each individual celebrity and appreciate the possibility that while some of them may have been launched into fame in spite of having no particular talents or admirable qualities, it is far from true that this is always or even fairly often the case. In addition, there is a tendency to see all celebrities as "fame seeking" when clearly this is not the case. Many celebrities, in fact, shun fame and try not to maintain a public profile. Christian Bale is a notable example of this, and there are many others.

Van Krieken (2012) makes a distinction that rather than celebrities being all alike, there is instead a uniform way that celebrity society as a whole shapes our behavior and the ways to which we relate to celebrities. It then becomes even easier to see celebrities as "all alike." The unique individuality of each celebrity gets lost in the complexity of celebrity society.

In an article on the sociology of celebrity status (Kurzman et al., 2007), it was observed that "sociologists, even sociologists who study celebrity, are not immune to its presence" (p. 355), and the researchers observed that "academics can be just as star-struck as anybody else" (p. 362). I have felt for some time that this has had a detrimental effect on the study and understanding of both celebrity and also fandom. Driessens (2015) wrote an article specifically about the challenges of interviewing celebrities that included similar observations.

In my years of getting to know various celebrities in a personal way, either as friends or as friendly acquaintances, I have found that most of those individuals do not meet the stereotypes of celebrities as craving fame, being materialistic, or being continually engaged in self-promotion.

## ALVIN TOFFLER: *THE THIRD WAVE*

It is important to consider the work of Toffler (1980) in describing the history of media and how in the 1980s we began the transition from a mass media world into a de-massified media world. Toffler's book *The Third Wave*, described three waves of change throughout human history: The first wave of change was from the hunter/gatherer society to an agrarian society where people stayed in one place and grew/raised their own food. In these two eras, there was no media. The second wave of change was from an agrarian society to an industrial society within which people moved from farms into cities and began to manufacture goods. At this time, the production of food became a more specialized industry. It was during the second wave of change that mass media was born and flourished.

During this era of mass media, it became possible to become known through means other than face-to-face interaction. An early form of media was books, and the power of words was such that phrases like "the pen is mightier than the sword" were born. Many 19th-century famous people were writers or writer/politicians, for example Mark Twain, Emily Dickinson, Abraham Lincoln, Frederick Douglass, and Charles Darwin.

Toffler proposed that the third wave of change began in the 1980s, and with it came subtle changes in the way we are affected by media. The de-massification of media heralded the dawn of a new age of media, and Toffler gazed into the near future and predicted quite accurately the saturation of media that was to take over. Rather than unifying society as did mass media, multiple forms of media and multiple media channels and outlets splintered one large market into a plethora of niche markets.

## THE POWERSHIFT TO INFORMATION AS POWER

Toffler (1990) also said that society was undergoing a powershift from a society where power was based on either physical strength or wealth to one where power came from information, as well as the already mentioned speculation that we had begun to move from a society dominated by mass media to one more characterized by de-massified media. There are a number of media phenomena involved. Television went from three or four central channels to cable television with dozens or even hundreds of choices. During the mass media era, everyone watched the same television. With the de-massification of media, choices were myriad and it would be far less usual for any two people to have seen the same television shows on any given day.

The same was true with magazines where the early and mid-20th century was characterized by a very small number of choices. There were a handful of highly influential magazines, read by almost every household, which included Life, Look, and The Saturday Evening Post. By the 1970s, circulation of the country's most popular magazines took a serious dive in number of readers, and what replaced them was a market of special interest publications that have comparatively small readerships. Television and magazines are examples of what Toffler meant by the de-massification of media. It was with the advent of the Internet and other digital forms of media that the de-massification of media really was complete. The media choices went from dozens to hundreds to thousands.

Toffler asserted that individuals create a storehouse of images in their consciousness, accumulated from birth. During the first wave, in the era of no media, children built their understanding of the world around them by taking in the real images of community with which they were surrounded. The second wave, with its infusion of media, multiplied exponentially the number of sources of images and information bombarding the child. In the process, a number of images were so pervasive that they become a part of the public psyche and were held in the minds of almost all people. An example might be the posters and images of "Uncle Sam" that were associated with recruiting during the World Wars. Such standardization of images and information during the second wave of change and the industrial age served well the goals of mass production and the factory model of the 18th, 19th, and 20th centuries.

## APPLYING TOFFLER

In the current third wave shift from mass media to de-massified media, where choices have multiplied, it has become far more difficult to become the household name superstar that characterized the 1950s through the 1980s. When The Beatles were on The Ed Sullivan Show on February 4, 1964, an estimated 73 million Americans saw their performance. Ed Sullivan was one of very few choices for television entertainment on Sunday evenings, and with this exposure, their popularity soared. Likewise, most households who owned a television set and enjoyed watching such entertainment saw the Jackson 5 on Ed Sullivan December 14, 1969, and again May 10, 1970. There were few television choices.

But with the splintering of media, the following of celebrities became a more specialized pursuit. I have pointed this out in my articles about the fandoms of Jackson 5 lead singer Michael Jackson, a fan group I followed closely from 1988 to 1992, and my subsequent study of the fans of Josh Groban from 2005 to the present (Stever, 2011a).

## JACKSON COMPARED TO GROBAN
## (PRE- AND POST-THIRD WAVE)

While Michael Jackson was signed with his first major record label, Motown, at about age 10, Josh Groban was discovered at the slightly older age of 17. Still both were very young when they were separated from the crowd. When Groban was 16 years old, he starred in his high school's production of *Fiddler on the Roof*, a performance so impressive that the first time Groban was a presenter for the televised Tony awards, producers trotted out the clip with him singing "If I Were a Rich Man" from that high school performance. Both artists were prodigies, recognized as exceptional talents from a young age.

The trajectories depart, one from the other, because Michael Jackson had a kind of media exposure in the '70s and '80s that wasn't possible by the year 2000, when Warner Brothers signed Groban and launched his career. If Josh Groban had been able to go onto a show like *Ed Sullivan* and sing for most of the television viewership of his day, he could have potentially become a bigger star. Instead, he had to reach small market after small market, first appearing on *Ally McBeal*, then singing the national anthem for the World Series, then finally appearing on the television program 20/20 where they profiled his career which resulted in his debut album climbing from 112 on Billboard's Hot 100 to 12 in one week. His talent hadn't changed, his voice was the same. However, more people saw him through this program, and his sales went significantly higher. Still 20/20 does not come close to having the audience that *The Ed Sullivan Show* had in the early 1970s. Groban built his career with help from a website and the Internet in general. In addition, he moved to a higher level of fame when he joined Twitter and started to build a following there. Talk shows like *Jimmy Kimmel Live!* and other late-night TV gradually increased his popularity.

By contrast, Jackson had *Ed Sullivan* in 1972 and 1973, and then starting in 1981, he had one of the first hit music videos on MTV. *Beat It*, *Billie Jean*, and *Thriller* all went on to be #1 hits, largely because of the popularity of the videos he made to go with those songs. In

1983 there was a TV special called Motown 25 celebrating the 25th anniversary of Motown that was carried by a major network. Nielsen estimated that 47 million people saw the program, representing 35% of the televisions in the country. On that show, Jackson did the "Moonwalk" and the country went wild. It is interesting that Jackson did not invent the Moonwalk; street kids had been doing it for years. What Jackson did was bring that move to a wider audience; it was something most of the United States had never seen, and we were blown away by it. That single show was later identified as a huge factor in Jackson becoming an even bigger star. Ultimately, Thriller has had over 50 million copies in sales and has been identified as the biggest selling album of all time.

Would Groban's unique voice and talent have made him into a bigger star if he had access to a wider audience? One can only speculate, but looking at similar voices in earlier eras – voices like Elvis, Sinatra, or even the earlier "crooners" like Robert Goulet or Mario Lanza – it seems likely. When Groban signed with Warner Brothers, most people who knew him thought he would sell a few albums and then go back to college to finish his music theater degree. Once it became clear that what he had was a marketable commodity (and due to the similar success of artists like Andrea Bocelli) a wave of singers with voices that were classically trained and sounded more like "serious singers" ultimately grew into American Idol and other "talent contest" shows. These produced such a wealth of Groban clones that people who did not know otherwise thought that Groban himself had gotten his start on American Idol, a misconception that I ran into with some frequency in the earliest days of my research on his fans (starting in 2005).

The arguments made here for Groban could easily be made in a similar way for other current stars like Lady Gaga, Katy Perry, or Justin Bieber who all have successful recording careers and are big stars, but are not household names as were Michael Jackson, Elvis, or The Beatles. It could also be argued that as celebrity as a commodity has grown, there are simply more choices and more competition, and audience members have a limited capacity to follow all of those available choices.

This discussion of the shift from mass media to de-massified media began with our discussion of Toffler, but all of the other theories mentioned in this chapter are affected by the changes in the forms of media available today. Parasocial attachments are easier to form with increased access to information about stars, as are attractions based on identification. With increased reciprocal interaction, the reciprocal determinism described by Bandura has more opportunity to come into play. A list of further reading on many of these theories that will enhance your understanding of how celebrity is explained. It is included at the end of this book.

# 3

## CELEBRITY VS. FAME

One of the problems in the academic study of celebrity is the lack of agreement on the meaning of terms. What exactly is fame, what is celebrity, and are they the same or are they different? While some scholars make a clear distinction between fame and celebrity, others use the terms as completely interchangeable (for example, Van de Rijt et al., 2013). While some scholars define celebrity as "the condition of being much talked about" (Luckhurst & Moody, 2005, p. 1), Braudy (1997) recounted that "in its root sense, fame means to be talked about" (p. 608). Is there any wonder that there is such confusion in the literature on celebrity?

This discussion will recognize the distinction proposed by Trevor Parry-Giles (2008), that celebrity and fame are distinct concepts, with fame being well known for having accomplished something extraordinary and celebrity being well known based on the promotion of one's personality (also see Cashmore, 2014). Thus, according to Rojek's categories (listed in Chapter 1), fame is "achieved celebrity," or being known for an important accomplishment. Ascribed (being born into fame) and attributed (being known for being well known) celebrity are the categories more associated with "celebrity" in a great deal of the literature. Again, the distinction is not held uniformly throughout all writings but is useful for this discussion.

The recognition of accomplishments that we associate with fame (and the "achieved celebrity" status that sometimes accompanies such recognition) is very much an expression of the particular social, economic, and political structures that exist in a given society at a specific period in its history. For example, Babe Ruth became famous (and then a great celebrity) based upon his extraordinary accomplishments as a baseball player. However, this recognition could only come at a point in time when the professionalization and commercial popularization of sports in America had become highly developed, as it had by the 1920s and 1930s when Babe became a sports hero. Had he been playing baseball in its earlier days in the mid-19th century when it was largely a local, amateur, or semi-professional activity, his talents would not have been so widely acclaimed.

As we look back through history, famous people, particularly before the advent of mass media, were people who had accomplished something extraordinary. However, as Boorstin (1961) pointed out, with the advent of media there was the tendency to create "pseudo-events" in order to bring attention to the people who want it. If, as Van Krieken (2012) has proposed, attention is a limited resource, then we have to be selective about where we invest our attention. Those who create pseudo-events, or events that are really only about the seeking of attention, are those for whom celebrity is the goal. If one wants fame, one tries to do something worth doing and then hopes to be noticed for it. If one really only wants celebrity, then any attention seeking behavior will do. There are also people who seek neither fame nor celebrity. What they receive is the result of things they do without hoping to receive attention. If you were Jonas Salk, and all you really wanted to do was prevent polio, then you pursued that goal without thinking in any way about personal gain; in fact in his lifetime, he was known to shun any attention to himself personally, although he did become a noted public figure in spite of that. Television personality Edward Murrow told Salk, "Young man, a great tragedy has befallen you, you've lost your anonymity," in recognition of the fact that Salk really didn't want to be known or famous (Glueck, 1980).

For some people, the pre-eminent goal seems to be material wealth rather than fame. Fame is a byproduct, as appeared to be the case with PT Barnum, a showman known for promoting various hoaxes. He sought attention for his spectacles in order to make money and became well known as a byproduct of those spectacles.

As mass media became more influential, personalities were valued for being average and relatable, rather than for being extraordinary. James Bennett's (2011) book on television personalities makes a clear distinction between those who portray someone else as opposed to those who portray themselves. Television personalities involve non-fiction programs and genres, things like talk shows, news programs, cooking shows, and game shows, places where we get to know the celebrity in that context. There is some overlap, as you have people like Oprah Winfrey who is both a talk show host and an actor.

Before mass media, most famous people were known for things they had done in their own real lives. The exception was stage actors who have been identified as the precursors to 20th-century movie stars (see Luckhurst & Moody, 2005). Radio personality Walter Winchell reported on the activities and lives of these "stars" with his focus being both Broadway and also the newly developing Hollywood motion picture industry. It was in this time period that modern celebrity society was evolving as contrasted with the earlier period of individually famous people, "achieved celebrities" such as Alexander, The Great or Julius Caesar.

There is a vast literature on celebrity and identification. Much of the value of the well-known person to audience members is as an anchor for identity. Who we are and what we stand for becomes clearer by using the famous person as a litmus test.

We will look at specific cases in order to understand what happens when fame comes first and then celebrity, or celebrity comes first followed by fame. There are also the less frequent cases where fame mostly exists without celebrity or celebrity exists without fame, again if one maintains that these are distinct albeit overlapping concepts.

## WHEN CELEBRITY PRECEDES FAME

When does celebrity precede fame? A clear example would be each of the 45 women who have been married to one of the presidents of the United States. These women had done little to earn fame before becoming first lady, but many of them went on to notable accomplishments after being thrust into the public eye.

### Abigail Adams

Abigail Adams lived from 1744 to 1818 in a time when women did not hold office or aspire to positions of leadership in the United States, and were not allowed to own property, publish their own writings, or in any way be much beyond someone's wife. Abigail Smith married John Adams when she was 19 years old in anticipation of living the ordinary life of a wife and mother. Their marriage and the subsequent events of the Revolutionary War created a situation wherein she was able to make important contributions to the early shaping of our country, both the founding of it and the recording of the historical events surrounding the birth of a nation.

Media creates celebrity, and this was true in all eras, not just beginning in the 20th century. The fame or achieved celebrity of Abigail Adams came from her role as first lady during a critical period of United States history. At a point towards the end of her life, the family realized the critical importance of the letters John and Abigail had written to one another, and they were careful to preserve those letters as an historical record of this time. Published in 1840 by her grandson, they were so popular that four editions of the volume were published. They remained a best seller well into the 19th century and her fame grew as a result. There were about 1,170 letters written mostly during the years when they were apart (1774 to 1784) due to John Adams' service to the country and Abigail Adams' service at home, as she not only raised their children mostly alone, but also became her husband's eyes and ears in the Boston area very near to where they lived. Although not particularly well known during her lifetime, she later was admired due to the influence of her letters and what they revealed about her role in the revolution and subsequent reconstruction of America.

As an example, she and her son, John Quincy (destined to become the sixth president of the United States), went to a vantage point where they could observe the Battle of Bunker Hill, and then Abigail recounted her observations in a letter to her husband, a letter that he shared with the Continental Congress. As an early champion of women's rights, an outspoken opponent of slavery and as an eyewitness to the revolution, Abigail Adams has become a revered persona in United States history. This is an example of how written media had the power to create celebrity in the time before media created celebrity society (Swain, 1982; Van Krieken, 2012). She exemplified being placed in a public position via her relationship to her husband, but later became famous in her own right.

In Chapter 1 we talked about Parry-Giles' article (2008) in which he accused biographer David McCullough of turning President John Adams into a celebrity, relying "on affective rhetorics of praise and admiration that dominate contemporary celebrity politics" (p. 88). It would appear that if one speaks about or makes known the achievements of a particular person, that focus qualifies the historical figure as famous or a person of renown. If one writes about the personal life or qualities of that historical figure, one has endowed this person with celebrity. Taking John Adams as an example, what makes McCullough's book so engaging is that he brings the characters in the story to life. One has read in history books about these prominent figures: Benjamin Franklin, Thomas Jefferson, John and Abigail Adams, and their son, John Quincy Adams. However, McCullough used the content of their already mentioned personal letters and succeeded in making them come alive by bringing attention to their personal qualities.

## WHEN FAME PRECEDES CELEBRITY: CHARLES LINDBERGH

Daniel J. Boorstin (1961) recounted the details of the case of Charles Lindbergh in his book, The Image. This is a clear case of someone accomplishing something remarkable, but then that accomplishment being eclipsed by the focus on his private life. In 1927, Lindbergh made the first transatlantic flight, New York to France, with much acclaim for his skill and bravery. A publicity campaign had been planned before his flight, inviting press attention. The flight was followed by several years of a rehashing in tens of thousands of words of news coverage. The press then focused on his marriage and the kidnapping and murder of his infant son. The feeding frenzy over all of this by news media made it difficult later to remember what it was he had done that had begun it all. What should have been an heroic life became tragic in the end.

Another example of fame coming before and leading to celebrity is Albert Einstein. During his lifetime, Einstein's accomplishments were not recognized right away; indeed, he had written many of his most important papers before he even received a professorship at a university. He worked in the patent office in order to make a living and was not particularly respected by others in his field until quite a bit later in his life. In the 21st century, Einstein is recognized as one of the most well-known names of the 20th century and many books have attempted to expose aspects of his private life and story, which is the hallmark of celebrity treatment. Time magazine recognized him as their "person of the century" and pointed out that his image and name were among the most instantly recognizable in the world. During his lifetime, Einstein was said to have achieved "celebrity" during his 40s and used his celebrity to promote Zionist causes, a move that was controversial among other Jews. While he would occasionally complain about fame, overall he embraced it and considered it something he had earned as a result of his work (Kennedy, 2016).

A difference between Lindbergh and Einstein is that while Lindbergh's accomplishment was almost eclipsed by his celebrity status, Einstein's was not.

## FAME TO CELEBRITY: ALEXANDER HAMILTON

In addition to John Adams, another example of a famous person who has been recently transformed into a celebrity and whose life has been sensationalized is Alexander Hamilton. Considered one of the "founding fathers" of the United States, Hamilton wrote the Federalist Papers and set up much of the US banking and financial systems, as he was appointed the first Secretary of the Treasury by George Washington. Hamilton remained in relative obscurity until 2015, when Lin-Manuel Miranda's Broadway musical debuted, a musical about Hamilton's life that caused a furor around him and many aspects of his private life. Also featured in the musical were the life and activities of Aaron Burr, another well-known founding father. Inspired by the 2005 biography, *Alexander Hamilton* by historian Ron Chernow, *Hamilton* became a huge Broadway sensation, sweeping the Tonys in 2016 and commanding ticket prices and sold out shows above and beyond any of its peers.

## CELEBRITY WITHOUT FAME: OSCAR WILDE

There are a number of 20th- and 21st-century examples of celebrity without much in the way of noteworthy accomplishment, but an earlier example illustrating that this is not just a current day phenomenon is the case of Oscar Wilde.

It was clearly Wilde's intention to become well known. David Friedman (2014) observed that "Wilde understood that perception is reality, and that image trumps the truth" (p. 144). Everything in Wilde's life was contrived to court attention from the public. He set out at a very young age to tour America and give lectures on various topics, but at this point in his life, he had accomplished little beyond a university education. He and his promoters billed him as an "expert" in aesthetics, and his talks were variations on the topics of art and beauty. One of his first acts in New York City was to have his portrait taken by Napoleon Saroney, one of the best known photographers of the day. These portraits became calling cards and advertising postcards that were printed and distributed to publicize the talks that Wilde was giving, talks that made money for both him and his promoter. One of the keys to his success was his tendency to dress in a manner that was outrageous and attention seeking.

While Wilde did eventually write a novel, several plays, and essays that are recognized as classics of modern English literature, he was originally best known for developing himself into what Boorstin (1961) called a "pseudo-event," something or someone noticed because of all the hype created around it/them. The subtitle of Friedman's biography is *Oscar Wilde and the Invention of Modern Celebrity*. If he did not actually invent celebrity, he certainly contributed to the idea that one could become well known for promoting oneself.

## FAME WITHOUT CELEBRITY: THE WRIGHT BROTHERS

The Wright brothers, Orville and Wilbur, through ingenuity, bravery, and persistence, invented the airplane, an event that changed the course of modern transportation. Reading David McCullough's (2015) biography, a number of things were striking about their story. Neither man attended college, although Wilbur had intended to go to Yale but recovery from a serious accident caused him to miss his opportunity. Orville opened a bicycle shop, and Wilbur joined him in the business, a venture that financed the work on their airplane. Like the story of John and Abigail Adams, what we know about their ongoing work comes from their letters to one another. Their commitment to aviation, their focus, and persistence is a great and heroic story of ingenuity. In this biography, there was little said about their personal lives, although it is clear that they had a close family and supported one another. Their sister Katherine, a schoolteacher who did go to college, played a critical role by being their public spokesperson during their time in France, deflecting the interest of the public and press, so that her brothers could focus on their work. She also nursed Orville back to health after his crash in September of 1908 and became his constant companion during his recovery period.

Once the Wright brothers had achieved flight, the press who wanted interviews and stories pursued them. They faced the same kind of public scrutiny that would befall anyone who has accomplished such an important feat. However, unlike Lindbergh, who sought out press coverage, the Wrights were careful and circumspect when giving interviews, and as already mentioned, had their sister run interference to keep the press away while they worked. Home from Europe in 1909, Dayton, Ohio, their hometown, threw a big celebration for them on June 17. This was the first formal recognition they received from Dayton for all they had accomplished. The brothers estimated that on that day, they had each shaken hands with about 5,000 people. The next day they were back at work on their flight trials. In fact, on the day of the celebration, they actually spent a fair amount of that day working on their current prototype. It would appear that fame didn't change them much. They never made a lot of money from their invention, living simple and austere lives. Wilbur died at age 45 of typhoid fever. Orville lived to be 76 years old and benefitted a bit more from material success, but still, while comfortable, was worth relatively little at his death. Clearly for these two men, "rich" and "famous" were not connected and not pursued.

## ICONS AND BRANDING

One result of the dominance of visual media in the 20th century was the celebrity icon. This is the celebrity represented by a visual symbol, e.g., the image of Albert Einstein, which has become synonymous with genius. This association is so strong that a large number of products have been marketed using the Einstein name, for example "Baby Einstein" or "Salesforce Einstein," a new line of artificial intelligence products designed to assist with customer success for that company.

Another term for this, particularly in the 21st century is "branding," meaning the creation of a trademark image as a way for people to market themselves or their ideas in an easy to remember "package." Michael Jackson had an image of himself in profile, up on his toes that was instantly recognizable to any who knew his name or career, which in the 1980s was pretty much everyone. Fictional characters like Mickey Mouse, Charlie Brown, or Homer Simpson have the same instant recognizability and association with a product (i.e., Disneyland) or a central trait. Charlie Brown as the insecure and down-on-himself little boy, or Homer Simpson as a bumbling and incompetent adult male are examples.

Branding as represented by these iconic symbols has become essential in a world where there is such an overload of information to process that people become overwhelmed. Celebrities become "brands" through a "Meaning Transfer Model" (McCracken, 1989, p. 307) that has three stages:

1 Celebrity is associated with meanings.
2 Meanings are associated with products.
3 Consumers take in these meanings by purchasing and using those products.

So, in our Einstein example, Einstein becomes associated with genius, high IQ, and academic status. Next the "Baby Einstein" product developers create an association between their products and the development of genius by labeling items with the *Baby Einstein* brand. Consumers buy these products believing that they are good for the cognitive development of their children.

## BRANDING IN POLITICS

Nowhere have the lines between celebrity and fame, or ascribed and achieved celebrity as some authors distinguish it, been so blurred as in the political arena. Ideally, one would like political leaders to be running things because of their past achievements and proven abilities as leaders. While this can happen, more and more frequently, the winner of an election is the one whose "brand" has been sold best to the public. In this context, the marketing of a candidate becomes more important than the actual realities of his or her achievements. Matthew Thomson (2006) asserted: "Celebrities can also be considered brands because they can be professionally managed and because they have additional associations and features of a brand" (p. 105).

There is no better example of this than with the brand of "Donald Trump" in the 2016 presidential election. Dumenco (2016) was correct when he asserted that Trump consistently presented himself as confident and tough even when his conclusions were wrong or even laughable. Although Trump's sound bites became instant fodder for new media critics and late-night talk shows alike, his behavior still reinforced his brand image. In this case, it is the image rather than any accomplishments or abilities that created the illusion that Trump was fit to be president. Part of the marketed brand for Trump was the notion that he stood for conservative ideology, something that made him attractive to the conservative evangelical right. In spite of the fact that Trump has been married three times, and has alleged extramarital affairs and sexual misconduct, his appearance of advocacy for conservative talking points such as pro-life or anti-gun control rhetoric have caused him to be supported by conservatives.

As in this example, the celebrity of a candidate has become the most important aspect of her or his ability to be elected rather than qualifications or demonstrated public interest. Rather than being public servants, elected officials all too often become public spectacles.

## BRANDING AND THE CELEBRITY AS A COMMODITY

Another ongoing discussion among scholars of celebrity is that of the celebrity as a commodity. The celebrity industry manufactures celebrities with only profit in mind (Turner, 2004). Writers and scholars question the authenticity of those in the public eye, alleging that the publicity machine capitalizes on "star quality" or charisma, cranking out bankable celebrities with little regard for any actual real talent or achievement. Taking a closer look at some examples, how universally true might this be?

While the endorsement value of prominent sports stars is marred if they misbehave (or worse) in public (for example, Tiger Woods or O.J. Simpson), their bankability is the result of the hard work and success that brought them to the public eye in the first place. Prominent athletes like Michael Jordan or Serena Williams would never have become media darlings with lucrative endorsement contracts without first getting to the top of their relative sports. While there is no question that the media publicity machine takes such talent and uses it for profit, the talent and hard work portion of the equation are aspects of celebrity that have been minimized in many writings on the subject. However, James Bennett (2011) has done a good job of describing the talent it takes to be a television personality.

Another theme in writings about celebrity is that celebrities are not showing their authentic or true selves when they appear in public. It's all an act, and the private self would never live up to the public self (Rojek, 2001; Turner, 2004). This is a trickier issue to address because as was already discussed, Goffman (1959) felt that every one of us is a player on the stage of life and the dramaturgical perspective on person perception says that we all play our ideal selves on this stage of life (see Chapter 2).

But because celebrities play themselves on a wider stage to a bigger audience than does the average person, the gap between the idealized self and the real self has the potential to become much wider for those who have achieved either fame and/or celebrity. Sue Bloland (2005, p. 7), writing about the life of her celebrity father, developmental psychologist Erik Erikson, said:

> Because of my father's celebrity, I have had an unusual opportunity to observe the way in which modern-day fairy tales are constructed around real-life people who have achieved fame. An idealized and oversimplified image is generated by the media – with the help of the celebrity, and the eagerly receptive public – an image with which people can easily identify and from which they can draw vicarious strength and inspiration. But such images are not realistic representations of human beings. On the contrary, they conceal the real complexity of the people around whom they are constructed.

So rather than being a false portrayal or "act" put on by the celebrity, the public image is an oversimplification of what the person's life is really like. It is not a conscious wish to mislead, but rather a desire to portray one's own life in a positive light, while still keeping personal complexities and challenges private.

## HEROISM

Another theme in some books on celebrity is that while historical figures are known for achievement, contemporary celebrities are simply media personalities with little to distinguish themselves except a complex marketing scheme to "sell" them to the public. Boorstin (1961) alleged that celebrities are "fabricated on purpose to satisfy our exaggerated expectations of human greatness" (p. 58).

When looking at such contemporary figures, it is not the lack of accomplishment but rather the media's glossing over of that accomplishment in favor of personal reports and scandals that makes the contemporary figure a celebrity rather than a person of fame according to this reasoning. It would appear then that being a celebrity is a construction of various media, just as being famous is also such a construction.

By bringing to light John Adams' personal foibles, and conflicts with others of the time, is it to be supposed that Adams has been transformed from an historical figure into a celebrity? This is no different from contemporary media focusing on the relationships, scandals, and personal qualities of, for example, the British Royal Family, someone like Princess Diana. Thus, her life is reduced to celebrityhood rather than her being acknowledged as an active philanthropist and spokesperson for various causes. The conclusion that this person is no longer the hero/role model that she might have been in a less mediated time seems unsupportable. It is the construction rather than the actual person that has changed over time. Perhaps what lacks depth of character and heroic substance is not the actual famous people of our time, but rather the way they are constructed in the media. The conclusion that we no longer have true heroes is difficult to accept.

The real problem for today is that in the celebritization of current leaders, we no longer judge them on their views or deeds, but rather on an emotional and affective evaluation of their personalities. This is a legitimate concern but one that appeared to be as valid during the time of John Adams as it is today. Adams was hampered in his work during the Revolutionary War by written communications accusing him of vanity and conceit and reporting him in a negative light. It would appear that written letters to Congress and other influential bodies of the time were the "tabloid influences" of the 1700s. If Congress lost its confidence in Adams' ability to negotiate for the country based on letters maligning him, how is this different from the voters losing confidence in a candidate based on things published about him or her in various news (or even tabloid) sources?

The key factor seems not to be the presence or absence of truly noble and heroic people but rather in all cases of how they are portrayed and how that portrayal is disseminated in the printed (and later visual) word. If, in fact, David McCullough (2002), through his biography, can turn John Adams into a celebrity, then how is any person of renown safe from such a process?

A few cases from current day celebrities will illustrate why I have always struggled with this dichotomy between fame and celebrity, and why I question that we have a lack of heroes in our time.

Keanu Reeves grew up with a father who had spent time in prison for selling drugs. His childhood was difficult for other reasons including his dyslexia, which caused him not to finish high school. In spite of this adversity, Reeves went on to star in such major hit films as the three *Matrix* films, *Speed*, and *The Lake House*. The following quote from IMDB (Internet movie database) is indicative of Reeves' thinking on the subject of fame and celebrity:

> I never cared about the money, that's not why I started acting, and I never liked the fame. The paparazzi culture is more pervasive than it used to be, kind of: 'Let's watch the actor pump gas.' It's nice not to have to worry about bills, though. It's a cliché that money doesn't buy you happiness, but it does buy you the freedom to live your life the way you want. Knock on wood, I've been very fortunate: I've been able to earn a really good living and start a charity foundation, which is nice.

*The Matrix* (1999), a very successful film with gross box office receipts of over $171 million (IMDB.com) was a success due in part to special effects and graphics such as had not been seen to that time in films. Reeves, for *The Matrix* sequels, reduced his box office take for those films in order to enhance the special effects budget. In like manner, he took a lesser salary in other films in order to ensure the success of those films, with money going to hire other cast members, etc. When his sister was diagnosed with leukemia, Reeves gave $5 million to leukemia research and founded a charity foundation supporting patients with cancer. He reportedly lives a low-key simple life, riding the subway in New York and forgoing many of the trappings of the celebrity lifestyle. He regularly supports other charities including Stand Up To Cancer, PETA, and the SicKids foundation (Lamare, 2014).

Another example of a philanthropic actor, one who turned adversity into philanthropy, was Christopher Reeve. Best known for his role as *Superman*, he was paralyzed in a horse-riding accident in 1995. He formed a partnership with the American Paralysis Association and through this connection, their revenue doubled in the next three years to $5 million. The charity was rebranded as the Christopher Reeve Foundation. Reeve was quoted on his own website as saying, "I think a hero is an ordinary individual who finds strength to persevere and endure in spite of overwhelming obstacles."

This quote describes both Christopher Reeve and Keanu Reeves as well as a dramatic 21st-century example of those heroic qualities in someone who has achieved both fame and celebrity. Malala Yousafzai (2013) was a young girl who was pursuing education in the Taliban infested country of Pakistan when she was targeted for speaking out on girls' rights to education, and she was shot in the face. Malala miraculously recovered from this attempted assassination and was relocated to England for her own safety and the safety of her family. She has written an autobiography describing her life before and after the attempt on her life, and in 2014 she was awarded the Nobel Peace Prize for her efforts in championing the rights of all children to education.

In this chapter, we have discussed a number of examples of celebrity and fame, analyzing the ways that fame can come before or after the public focus on one's personal life. The variety of men and women in this discussion highlights the fact that, as I have maintained all along, celebrities of all types are each unique individuals who cannot be grouped into any kind of homogenous category. Time in history, gender, age, accomplishments, motivation, and intention all play into each individual example.

# 4

---

# CHALLENGES OF LIFE AS A CELEBRITY

How does celebrity affect the celebrity? Whether or not fame is embraced or rejected, it has a big effect on those who have the experience. For this chapter, I asked my celebrity friends about their experiences and also read celebrity autobiographies.

The celebrities I know quite well are from my association with *Star Trek*. *Star Trek* is its own little world where a number of people are famous yet outside of that world they are not well known. However, most of those I interviewed had experiences outside of *Star Trek*. Rene Auberjonois, in particular, was already well known before he was cast for *Star Trek* in his 50s, having had an extensive Broadway, film, and television career. Siddig (stage name Alexander Siddig; family name Siddig El Fadil) had grown up in a family that included Uncle Malcolm McDowell, a ruling class family in Sudan, and his stepfather, Sir Michael Birkett, a member of the House of Lords. Tea at their home in the years I knew Michael involved anecdotes about George Solti, Margaret Thatcher, and other famous people. Andy Robinson had the particularly life changing experience of being Scorpio, the famous villain from *Dirty Harry*. Armin Shimerman played numerous television parts outside of *Star Trek* including *Beauty and the Beast* and *Buffy the Vampire Slayer*. Chase Masterson was on *General Hospital* before being cast for *Star Trek*. All of these actors are from theater backgrounds and are well educated, so it could be argued that they are not representative by any means of all celebrities, or even television celebrities. Still their experiences reflect what it is like to be someone who is recognized on the street by strangers and to whom people will pay money for an autograph.

## VALUES

What matters to a person, his or her values, has a fundamental impact on how that person reacts to being famous. Schwartz (2012) has identified 10 basic values that guide the way people live their lives. They are self-direction, stimulation, hedonism, achievement, power, security, conformity, tradition, benevolence, and universalism. All of these relate to the concept of celebrity and how celebrity is sought, achieved, and valued once it is achieved. What one chooses to do with celebrity once it is obtained can be anticipated by what the individual values, indeed whether or not fame is desired is a function of values. Some who pursue celebrity have as their motivation the more stereotypical notion of wanting to be "rich and famous" and this would reflect hedonism, achievement, power, and security, all things that might come with fame.

Ava Gardner's (1990) autobiography reflects an individual who grew up in an extremely poor family so that when she arrived in Hollywood with the promise of a steady income, a glamorous lifestyle, and beautiful clothes to wear (actors had access to the entire wardrobe at MGM for public appearances), she embraced all of these things, happy to have achieved security. Later in her life, she experienced the loss of privacy that is characteristic of the superstar celebrity. She recounts her marriage to Frank Sinatra and being unable to get away from the press. Their wedding was held in a private home, but information that was leaked such that the entire press corps was on the front lawn the day of the wedding. Her situation was so difficult that she finally moved to Spain, just short of her 33rd birthday.

> Why did I go? For one thing, for as long as I lived there, I'd never liked Hollywood. . . . It was more and more impossible to have

any privacy there. I couldn't walk my dog, go to an airport or a restaurant, I couldn't even go to the ladies room without somebody around watching me, reporting on me, spying on me. I felt imprisoned by the lifestyle of a movie star, and I just couldn't live with that anymore.

(p. 219)

Arthur Miller (2013), arguably the most famous playwright of the 20th century (*Death of a Salesman*, *The Crucible*), also married to Marilyn Monroe, talked in his autobiography about the irony of having achieved success by writing about a difficult life of pain and failure.

As a success I was occasionally greeted by people on the street with a glazed expression that was pleasant but made me feel unnervingly artificial. My identification with life's failures was being menaced by my fame.

(p. 138)

He lamented what he saw as an inevitable touch of arrogance that accompanies fame:

[S]uch an order of recognition imprints its touch of arrogance, quite as though one has control of a new power to make real everything one is capable of imagining.

(p. 193)

However, early in his career, he was not willing to compromise his values for material gain:

My purity was still breathtakingly unmarred through the thirties, so much so that at a certain point in 1939, only months out of college and conniving to get myself a twenty-three-dollar-a-week job on the Federal Theatre Project. . . . I had no qualms about turning down a two-hundred-and-fifty-dollar-a-week offer by . . . Twentieth Century Fox, to come work for them.

(p. 231)

Clearly, materialistic motivations are not a universal trait of those who pursue success and influence in their artistic realm. My actor interviews below show that being famous did not automatically mean becoming rich and wasn't the highest value or goal in most cases.

Self-direction is often sacrificed in the pursuit of fame, and a number of celebrities (e.g., Ava Gardner, 1990) report that they became victims of the "star system" by being exploited and manipulated in an environment where getting the role was so very important. This is a particular issue for women as Chase Masterson talks about in her interview later in this chapter. If you become famous enough, you become more able to reclaim self-direction and also power over both yourself and others. On the Madonna Blonde Ambition tour in 1990, in my interviews with fans, many reported that the way she had taken over control of her career was what they admired about Madonna. In the interview with Keanu Reeves quoted in Chapter 3, it was clear that having achieved success and fame had given him the freedom to do the projects he wanted to do. Armin Shimerman also mentions how being well known opens up new roles for him in theater.

I asked these actors from Star Trek: Deep Space Nine (DS9) when they became aware of their own celebrity and how this affected their lives.

## ARMIN SHIMERMAN

I met Armin Shimerman in 1994 at a Star Trek convention. In 1998 as the show was ready to wrap, we did an interview where we discussed things relevant to fans and celebrity; I asked him if he had any particularly fond memories of the fans of the show:

> Two encounters with fans stand out in my mind. One was a young man in a wheelchair who was just terrific and touched my heart. I was able to get him on the stage at the convention. It was nice to see a dream come true for him. I was particularly moved by that. The other special memory: We were shooting at Quark's and the sound stage was filled with smoke. You could barely see your hand in front of your face. I was standing with

Judi Brown, the script coordinator, and out of the smoke came a wheelchair with Stephen Hawking with Rick Berman right behind him. I remember that just took my breath away. I have always been a major fan of Stephen Hawking and one feels small next to his brilliance. And there he was! Rick (Berman) told me he had come particularly to see me.

More recently, I asked Armin about the point where he realized he was a celebrity:

A definition of "celebrity" is that it is "The condition of being widely known and esteemed; a (popular) public figure." If I were to admit it to myself, I would have to accede that I am a public figure. My existence is acknowledged in many parts of the world. The debatable part is whether I am esteemed. A man pulling trapped people from a burning car is to be esteemed; a leader for civil justice and an advocate for others is to be esteemed; a care-taker for the elderly and the infirm is to be esteemed. My popu-larity is from none of those and I have never thought the large mass of actors do anything extraordinary, though I will admit some performances are life-changing. Film/TV actors are just public craftsmen who insinuate themselves into people's minds via pixels in living rooms, magazines, and darkened theaters. So, rather than say, "I am a celebrity," I will answer that I am aware that I am a public figure.

My first awareness of that was my first convention where I was feted for being on *Beauty and the Beast* (a United States television series that ran from 1987 to 1990). It was humbling to be the focus of so many people's interest in my performance as Pascal. Here was a room full of people applauding what I had done and significantly educated/eager to know about my acting choices. Prior to that I had acted in a void and was totally unaware of what effect I was having on others. But that was only a hundred or so people in Birmingham, England. The next road marker on the way to awareness was being chosen to be the cover on the

*TV Guide.* Here was an esteemed institution suggesting that I was popular enough (or at least my *Star Trek* character was popular enough) to attract attention and sell thousands of magazines. The last argument for my acceptance of my popularity was the recurring occasions when people would stop me in the street. All three of these were instrumental in convincing me that I am "widely known."

On the positive side, there is a great endorphin of well-being that arises from being appreciated and in some ways applauded for work done. I am sometimes told my performances helped people through hard times. That is the most positive side of my popularity. In a business that teems with self-love and self-aggrandizement, these messages of thanks keep me humble and more appreciative of the things I have done. Needless to say, there is also the positive effect of getting better and quicker attention from service people who recognize what I have done in my profession. Though much rarer now, in the past, my popularity often allowed me to skip auditions and just be offered roles. Avoiding the angst of being judged was a scenario "devoutly to be wished."

On the negative side, my popularity from mainly Sci-Fi shows has pigeonholed me in my career aspirations. If I walk into an audition room and someone tells me how much they love my work, I can be guaranteed that I will not get a role that diverges from those iconographic characters. Thus, I am not considered for more subtle and dramatic characters because my popularity deems me unfit to embody that set of characters. When I was younger and an unknown face, it was easier to compete for roles. They simply judged me by what I brought into the room and not by a host of performances that trailed behind me. I was not recognized and pigeonholed immediately. More because the majority of my roles have been on TV, there is still a prejudice against popular TV character actors migrating to films. I believe my success in one media has hurt me in the other. Happily, I have learned to use my popularity to gain access to more theater productions, where my popularity can be an asset.

Almost as bad is the difficulty dealing with people who know me first and foremost as an actor. People are less forthcoming and more shy when they are afraid to be themselves in front of someone they recognize. Conversely, people can invade your privacy all too easily when they simply want to "come over and say hello." Then I am obliged to be charming and slightly talkative because they are offering a compliment by recognizing me.

I asked if there was any impact of his celebrity on loved ones?

Most definitely. I am married to an exceptional woman who is successful in so many arenas. Yet, if we are introduced to new people and I am recognized for my work by them, Kitty is often relegated to the side-lines and neglected. Unless I immediately become her advocate, she is often treated insignificantly as "the wife" or "the lesser actor." In addition, my success has sometimes made my very talented wife feel that she has had a lesser career than me, despite the fact she knows herself to be an extraordinary actress and I know what great work she has done. Further, my early success was at times tough on my brother who bore the brunt of having a "celebrated" brother. Sibling rivalry reared its ugly head and he was left feeling slightly inadequate in comparison. Both my brother and my wife have long since become inured to those slights, but I am still grieved when they occur.

## SIDDIG EL FADIL, AKA ALEXANDER SIDDIG

Siddig El Fadil was cast in DS9 in 1992 and achieved overnight celebrity, as does anyone who is cast as a regular character on Star Trek. He had the shortest resume of the cast regulars and was a complete unknown to the American television audience. His uncle, Sadiq Al Mahdi, is the deposed prime minister of Sudan, a country where Siddig was born and lived until he was 4. Moving to England with his mother, he continued to have contact with his ruling class family. When his mother remarried, Siddig's stepfather was Sir Michael

Birkett of the House of Lords. By the time Siddig had been cast for *Star Trek*, he had already dealt with fame on multiple fronts.

In 1993, I met Siddig in the midst of my graduate work in fan studies at a *Star Trek* convention. He granted me, over the course of the show, 11 extensive interviews. He talked about having fans for the first time in April of 1993 when only a few episodes of *DS9* had aired thus far. He started off that interview by saying:

> I didn't really mean to become an actor, so whatever comes along with that I find quite ordinary, at least to the extent that I've got people in my family who've been stars and I've noticed what happens to them.

At that early point of the show he was having fan mail delivered to his trailer at work every two or three months (averaging about 10–15 pieces of fan mail a day). A great deal of that mail was simply requests for autographs, but in and amongst those requests were very personal letters, or people asking him things, some in his role as a doctor on *Star Trek*. He recounted to me that he had been warned of the fans as being "incredibly mad" so after his first convention he came to the realization that most fan behavior was actually quite normal and ordinary.

> Hearing about people all dressed up in *Star Trek* uniforms and families turning up in *Star Trek* uniforms is bizarre! It's much more bizarre on paper than it is in life, because in life you realize that they're actually quite normal and it's just a fun sort of get-together thing.

I asked him about an interview he had done for *Starlog* magazine where he had said he didn't expect much attention from his role in *Star Trek*:

> Yes, that was serious and I'm still not sure what to expect. I'm so un-Hollywood, so unlikely to be in Hollywood, not a typical

actor to be here by any means. I can easily walk down the street and am recognized about twice a day. You can also walk down the street and not be recognized if you don't want to be. At this point, I don't find it annoying.

Siddig and also Rene Auberjonois were among several actors who didn't want fan clubs because, as Siddig said:

I had always thought fan clubs were just a place where you bought merchandise and that was not my idea of fun. I never really understood the whole adulatory thing and never did like that.

Both of these actors as well as several of the other DS9 actors agreed to have official fan clubs when they realized that there was charity fund raising potential in organizing a fan club.

In 1996, reflecting on the earlier interview from 1993, Siddig said:

My experience has been very different to (his uncle) Malcolm's but then I don't have the same degree of celebrity that he has. The difference is that because it's Star Trek, it's very isolated. You know exactly where the trouble is. You go into a room and there are 3,000 people there who are Star Trek fans. Once you leave they aren't there anymore. They get distributed amongst the sea of people out there most of whom aren't Star Trek fans. It's not like being a movie star where everyone has seen this movie so every-one in some form or another has a piece of you. So, it's much easier because it's contained.

In an earlier interview, Siddig had said "L.A. is a carnivorous city. It will eat you if you let it." I asked him if this still was true.

Yes, that's (still) true. L.A. will eat you if you let it and it does, countless young actors and actresses every day who end up over-dosing on some horrific drug. I do see myself as a Hollywood actor now and I'm kind of used to that. I found out that you can be a Hollywood actor and not be what I used to think of as a Hollywood actor. . . . I would think of someone who is self-aggrandizing, someone who lived for the publicity coup, who acted for Hollywood's sake as opposed to for their own. There's a difference between being an actor to being a star, which is perfectly reputable if you're into that sort of thing. People like Demi Moore or Arnold Schwarzenegger act to be stars and they do very well at it. That's where the bucks are. But you get the other kind of actor who acts because they like it and because they see it as a valid way of communicating things to people. So you see those actors in Susan Sarandon or Tim Robbins. You can clearly see the difference between the (two) kinds of actors we're talking about. One has to be able to "play the game" of being a star, at least in terms of self-promotion in order to say anything at all. You've got to get in to get it out. I'm probably trying to balance both of those two things, the self-promotion and the serious acting.

When asked if fame was any more invasive than it had been four years earlier he replied, "No, I can still do whatever I want to do."

In our final interview as the show was getting ready to wrap in late 1998, Siddig made some observations about the show and the fans:

I've seen literally thousands of fans and seen them up close and personal. The fans I meet are a perfect cross section of the population. I have fond memories of the fans and I have watched them as they have watched me. At our private fan club parties, I was able to turn up and just be me without all the regimented convention structure and bodyguards and that was nice. So, I got to know the fans and think differently about them than a lot of the press do.

In early 2018, Siddig answered some questions for me about his experience with celebrity in the 20 years since the end of the show.

First, I asked, "At what point in your career did you realize you were a celebrity?"

That's a difficult question to answer as my instinct has always been to avoid the spotlight if at all possible. I've never had a publicist, for example. I was often warned about how my life was about to change when I arrived at Paramount Studios in 1992, but those words seemed like so much hot air. However, if I were to point to one moment when I realized that there was no avoiding a certain amount of attention it would be during a visit to Disneyland in the mid 1990s with my young stepson, Buster. Apart from the very welcome offer to jump the lines, it wasn't until we went downstairs to meet Mickey Mouse where the young man inside the suit broke his vow of silence (and the magic for the other kids patiently waiting for a hug) by blurting out, "My God, it's Dr. Bashir!"

A very few actors, no matter what they do, cannot avoid the glare of publicity. However, most seek it out in some way – for good reason – the better known you are the higher the price you can command. Actors like me (mid ranked, I suppose) have a choice: either we can choose to drive the Ferrari, sure to turn heads, or we can jump in the little Toyota and be ignored. I guess you know that you're a celebrity when you're in the compact and still turn heads. The other sure way to know that you've become different is when you travel. It's not many people who land at an airport in a country they've never visited before and encounter people who already know who you are. Star Trek was sold in dozens of countries and people would stop to say "hi" from Paris to Aman.

What were the impacts, both positive and negative, on your life when this happened?

There are very few negative impacts if the only thing people know you for is your actual body of work. The occasional person becomes so fixated that they try anything to be around you – I've encountered several people (usually much younger girls) who would travel round the world to see me at an event, one girl who told her mother that she was visiting friends but turned up in my elevator in Vegas, for example. I'd already spent time with her (and her mother) when they came to see me in Spain. The problem was that this girl was Irish and must have spent a fortune. She wrote me maybe 20 times a day on a Facebook page that I had set up especially to deal with her. Eventually I was forced to ignore her completely. Another young woman turned up at my house in Sussex – she was Dutch.

I guess people think they know me, and in a way they do, but it's pretty confusing when they have trouble understanding that not only do I not know them but have no particular interest in starting a relationship.

I think things would have been a lot worse if I had shared more of myself with the public. We once invited a magazine into our Los Angeles house to take pictures of us at home – nothing good came of it but we did get some emails we had to pass to the FBI they were so racially charged and threatening.

Was there any impact, either positive or negative, on your loved ones?

On the one hand, being a familiar face gives me a free pass to friendly relations with complete strangers. Once someone knows me from the screen they treat me as a friend. The same thing has probably happened to my son; he doesn't mind telling me that he has several friends who follow my career or are fans of a particular show or movie. I think it must be mildly thrilling for my wife or anyone else I spend time with when people walk up to us in the street and praise me for a performance or thank me for a contribution I have made to their life. It's always great to feel welcome. I know I like it when I'm with a friend who gets recognized and effusively congratulated. It's certainly more relaxing to bask in someone else's sunshine than my own.

I can't think of anything truly negative – perhaps the fact that people think I must be fabulously wealthy is an irritation.

You have the added experience of prominent people in your family being quite famous from your Uncle Malcolm to your uncle the prime minister and your stepfather the member of the House of Lords and his many friends.

My uncle Malcolm's experience is different to mine – he is a much brighter star and has to be more careful. He's also a very different personality and when he was young and a household name took full advantage of his renown, living "the life." I probably behave the way I do because I saw how complicated life can easily become if you fly close to the flame. I'd prefer a smaller pay check any day.

Prime Ministers (referring to his Uncle Sadiq) lead a different existence altogether. Their security is paramount even long after they lose office – in effect they become metaphorical nuns, forever in the monastery of their own fragile vulnerability. They can change people's fortunes with the stroke of a pen and relations must always be colored by that knowledge.

My stepfather was one of the last hereditary peers in England, and although he deserved some respect for his formidable achievements, I think he also enjoyed respect from some people because of his title. On the one hand, that's the point of a title but there is an uncomfortable relationship with history and class in the UK. My half-brother Tom is a young Baron in his thirties – he prefers to be called just Tom even though he's supposed to be called, "your Lordship" or some such antiquated nonsense.

At the end of the day, I think I feel sorry for the big stars I have known. Whether it's (George) Clooney or (Matt) Damon, British royalty or Sudanese political figures – they all have one thing in common – they will never make friends the way normal people do. They will never bump into a complete stranger and carve out a relationship through mutual respect and fondness, because the scales have already been tipped and the essential process of co-discovery will always be absent. I still have a chance to meet people who don't know who I am, but it only takes a couple of minutes to go online and upset the natural pace and balance of knowledge.

## CHASE MASTERSON

In the third season of DS9, Chase Masterson came on the show as the popular recurring guest star, Leeta, the Dabo girl. On the first day she was filming, many male employees of the show found excuses to go to the set to watch her film. Chase is a very beautiful woman, and the story arc created for Leeta was among the most interesting on the program. By the end of the show, her character had married Rom, the Ferengi, having passed on all the traditionally handsome characters, playing out a sort of "Beauty and the Beast in Space" tale.

Chase has had a long relationship with her *Star Trek* fan club and their first charity was *Caring for Babies with Aids*, a care center based in Los Angeles. It was impressive that she didn't just raise money, but she would go and rock the babies and be there with them. She was the founder of the *Pop Culture Hero Coalition: Let's Stop Bullying Together*. Their website states their mission: "Founded in 2013, we are the 1st-ever 501c3 organization to use stories from TV, film & comics to make a stand for real-life heroism over bullying, racism, misogyny, LGBTQ-bullying, cyber-bullying, and other forms of hate."

I asked her if she thought there were issues in becoming a celebrity that were unique to women:

> As we've seen with the #MeToo movement, there has been an incredibly horrific number of women who have come forward to say they had been in abusive situations. On some level, movies can inspire us to be the best we can be, and they are about authentic connection, justice, integrity, compassion . . . to think that while those movies were being made, women were being subjected to everything from propositions to actual assault is horrifying.

I asked her about issues raised in *The Beauty Myth* (Wolf, 2013), a book about lookism in the media:

> So many have been led to believe that their looks were the most important thing for their careers and they're wrong. It's a lie

that is perpetuated by the industry as a whole. It's easy to get trapped into that way of thinking unless you make it a point to find an identity or create an identity and a sense of self apart from your looks.

I asked her about any negative aspects to being a celebrity, and she talked about an incident in her early career where she had been the victim of stalking by a fan.

It happened right after DS9 ended in November of that year, and it was horrific and life changing. A fan listed me on an international dating site with all my personal information without my permission. The horror of what happened was life changing in the worst possible way. It led to painful things. The bottom line is it was paralyzing. I can't get back the time that I lost being paralyzed. It could embitter me if I let it, but I can't. I have opportunities now that help me to heal and be more compassionate. Women have incredible opportunities to use their pain for good that we don't use often enough.

There are other aspects of acting that make celebrities vulnerable, and Chase recounted, as had the others, the frustration of being typecast:

I couldn't get cast as anything but a Dabo girl . . . being typecast is something that a lot of us deal with.

But she also said that incidents like being stalked and also looking around the world at places where people have no drinking water or where they live in terrible conditions puts something like that frustration into perspective. There are worse things than being typecast as an actor.

Talking about the fans who come to conventions to see her and hear her stories she said:

It's about understanding why people come to conventions and understanding why fans connect with Star Trek. You have to go back to the heart of it. They want to meet us because they connect with these stories and characters. The basic truth is that it is not about us. It's about the transcendence of these stories. The point is getting back to the humanity of these stories and the power these stories give. What is it that makes fans love this show? What makes them show up to meet us and hear our stories at conventions? Actors who think it is about us as individuals are deluded. The stories transcend and have life changing values.

She felt fortunate to have been given the love story between Leeta and Rom as a way to show that who a person is on the inside is what really matters. "Doesn't everyone want to be loved for who they are regardless of what is on the outside?"

She summed it all up by saying:

The important thing to realize is that celebrity is not what makes us happy in life. Yes, there are perks that come from it, but it's not what wakes me up in the morning. Friendships, family, health, and our own personal missions to make the world a better place is what is most important.

## RENE AUBERJONOIS

I remember the first time I saw Rene Auberjonois in person. My brother and I were attending the largest Star Trek convention of the year in 1993, and I remember thinking "What a nice man! I would love to meet him some day!" Several years later, we were working together at a charity event, and I recounted that anecdote to Rene and he said, "Wow, and now you're one of my dearest friends!" This comment is reflective of the kind and generous spirit that is Rene Auberjonois. One of the things that stands out about him is his untiring efforts for charity. Rene, as well as the other actors interviewed here, saw Star Trek and the energy of that audience as a chance to do significant work for their favorite charities. Over a period of nine years (1994 to 2003), these actors in collaboration with their fan clubs, and supported by the other members of their cast, raised over $350,000, donated to their various charities.

Rene had been a big star long before DS9. In 1970, he had starred on Broadway with Kathryn Hepburn in the musical Coco and won a Tony for that role. He had three other Tony nominations and many leading roles on Broadway, more recently starring with Michael Crawford in Dance of the Vampire (2003). Then there was his film career. He has done a number of prominent film roles including Mash and The Patriot, and his list of television credentials is in the hundreds including series regular parts on Benson, DS9, and Boston Legal.

I asked him when he was first aware of his own celebrity status. He recounted that his earliest memory of being recognized was from a play he had done in the Arena theater in Washington, DC. He and his wife Judith were traveling in Rome and were approached by someone who had seen his work in that play. It was to be the first of many times that he would be approached and recognized.

He recounted a particularly interesting incident:

> I was doing a play that was about to open on Broadway and we were trying the show out of town. The show starred Mikael Baryshnikov (Kafka's Metamorphosis in 1989). We had been in North Carolina, at Duke University, and were in the airport on the way back to New York. Many people started coming up to us and many of them recognized me first because I had done Benson and been on national TV. He thought that was very funny and was amused by the fact that he was a superstar and more people were recognizing me. That was the power of television. If we had been in New York City everyone would have recognized Baryshnikov, but in North Carolina, I was more recognizable.

Indeed, it was in airports that people would often approach Rene, but what would happen was that they would think he looked familiar and that they must know him from somewhere. Rene refers to himself as a "character" actor and as such, his face is well known to people, but they often can't recall his name. After trying to remember where they had met, Rene would tell those who persisted that he had been on television and then it would "click" for the person and they would recognize him for his work. Because he isn't a "superstar" the number and nature of such incidents is rarely invasive, and he said he found it mostly flattering to have people come up and tell him that they had enjoyed his work.

When I asked him if there were any negatives or downsides to being a celebrity, he replied:

> I have had a number of friends who are huge celebrities, for example Henry Winkler at the peak frenzy of being The Fonz on Happy Days. I've worked with Richard Dreyfuss, and we were working together when he won the academy award (1978, The Goodbye Girl), so I am very aware of the drawbacks of that kind of celebrity. You can't go to the supermarket or out to dinner because you are constantly being approached and people move into your space. I've never really had to deal with that to that extent. I remember once here in New York City I was doing Benson, and my son and I (he was maybe 10 years old) went out to have breakfast in a diner. A man came up and was encroaching on our space, wanting to sit down at the table with us, and I had to politely tell him that my son and I were having some time together and he went away. My son asked if I knew him and I said "no." . . . It disturbed my son that a total stranger would come up to us and act as if he knew us.

We talked about working on Broadway and the current tendency for big name stars to come out after shows and sign autographs or pose for "selfies." Rene recalled how Katherine Hepburn had protected herself and her privacy and not interacted with the public or signed autographs in this way. The opportunity to perform in a more intimate setting of 2,000 or fewer in the audience helps the actor feel more of a connection with that audience with whom they have just had this intimate experience. For those who do it, coming out to sign is a response to that interaction, one that big name actors like Jake Gyllenhaal or Josh Groban or Hugh Jackman don't often get to make. Along these same lines, Rene talked about a recent cruise he had been on where he had done readings with Nana Visitor, and a simulated radio show produced by John DeLancie. While he enjoyed all the fans coming up and saying "I enjoy your work," the ones who came up and said "I saw you last night in DeLancie's *Scopes* radio show" were particularly welcomed as again, this was a chance to share an intimate audience experience with someone who had just seen his work.

Indeed, the *Star Trek* convention was an opportunity to hear from the television audience in a way that usually doesn't happen.

> When *Star Trek* began, you could go out and actually meet your fans in a setting like a convention. When you perform on TV and film, the audience is anonymous, but actually to encounter the audience that has been supporting you, that is what encourages actors to be even more willing to interact with fans than they might already have been.

Speaking about how location is a big factor in the experience of being a celebrity:

> Part of how you deal with celebrity has to do with where you are. If you are in New York City or in Hollywood, most of the population that you encounter in those major entertainment centers (excepting the tourists) accept the fact that they live in a city with lots of celebrities. When I walk around New York City, people will recognize and acknowledge me, give me a thumbs up or something, but they don't try to interact because they accept the fact that they are in this big city where celebrities live and move and they give them more freedom. If you are in a small town somewhere, before you know it you can have 15 people standing around because that one person who recognizes you telegraphs it to everyone who is nearby.

We talked about how social media and the Internet might be changing fan/celebrity interaction:

> I feel a responsibility to those who have chosen to follow me on Twitter. I am very aware that those followers are real people and I feel a responsibility and will tell them if I decide to stop. I can reach out to my fans on there because there aren't an overwhelming number of them. If I were Beyoncé, I wouldn't be able to do that. There would be too many.

One of the ways Rene interacts with fans is through his website, *Renefiles*, run by his fan club organizer, Marguerite Krause. One of the things she does is collect questions from fans and when she has several, she sends them to Rene and he sends back answers. The Internet provides new avenues for a fan to ask a celebrity a question that didn't exist 15 to 20 years ago.

The new emphasis on social media can have a down side as illustrated by a friend of Rene's who was up for a role, and the producer of the show was excited to use him, but the television network decided that this person didn't have enough Twitter followers. However, on the plus side, Rene's son Remy was getting ready to publicize the film he had made (*Blood Stripe*), and Rene's 77,000 plus followers on Twitter were useful in helping that cause.

Rene concluded our interview by saying: "There are different aspects of celebrity. When you talk about the Kardashians versus Christopher Plummer, it's apples and oranges."

## ARON EISENBERG

Aron Eisenberg is an actor whose celebrity came from being on *DS9*. Aron told me he didn't see himself really as being a celebrity or very famous, even though (as I pointed out to him) a large percentage of people (54% in one poll) in the United States self-identify as *Star Trek* fans. Another aspect of Aron's fame on the show is affected by his wearing a prosthetic mask for most of the time he is on screen (he had one episode out of his 47 where he appeared without the prosthetic Ferengi head). Aron told me that he can walk through large *Star Trek* conventions without many people recognizing him, although just as many do from his appearances on stage at conventions and the many autograph lines where fans seek his autograph or a photo.

Additionally, Aron has a social media presence on Twitter and Facebook and also co-hosts an Internet talk show called *The Alpha Quadrant*, one he does with Garrett Wang of *Star Trek Voyager*. He told me that he feels that his celebrity in the *Star Trek* convention world comes as much from him being very social, reaching out to fans, as it does his work on the show, and this is most likely true. I have seen Aron at the big Las Vegas *Star Trek* convention several times, and at each one, he chats with fans, signing and selling his photographs, as he has a photography business and his very artistic photographs are something special.

One of the interesting aspects of Aron's celebrity is something that happened in late 2015. As a teenager, he had been the recipient of a kidney transplant and in 2015, that kidney quit functioning and he had to seek another donor. Responding to that Aron said:

> Look at all the love and financial help I received with my kidney transplant because of *Star Trek*. I don't know what I would have done. It happened so fast and there was no chance to plan. I don't know what I would have done without everybody's help.

Aron is referring here to the fact that fans contributed to a gofundme account to help him out during the time when he suddenly needed that transplant. It was a dear fan/friend who donated the kidney.

Going on to talk further about his experience of being a celebrity:

> I don't overall see myself as a celebrity. I guess I'm famous to some degree because people appreciate meeting me, the person who played Nog. So I've been introduced to being, in a small way, a celebrity. But, I think of myself more as a working-class actor. I worked as a server when I wasn't on the show. I've always had to have my business and part time jobs to have income between

acting jobs in order to give me freedom to do the acting I wanted to do. I was blessed to be part of the *Star Trek* world and outside of that, people don't really know who I am. People know me because I'm sociable at the conventions. I've never really had a huge thing about being a celebrity but it's awesome when people like my work.

Most actors have a life that is peaks and valleys. The majority of us come from a working class background and we go back and forth because we have to pay the bills. Once it is in the public's mind that you are a celebrity, they think of you as "Hollywood Elite," and that isn't true at all. Others think you are part of that, and have a preconceived idea of who they think you are if you are a "Hollywood Actor."

I asked Aron if having controversial political views on social media had brought him negative attention in any way:

Being controversial politically, I don't think it's hurt me at all, if anything it's gotten me more Twitter followers. Most of those who follow me seem to agree with my views, although the few that don't agree do seem to hang in there with me. That all was made available because I was a *Star Trek* celebrity. People are key-board warriors. . . . They say whatever they want without fear of repercussions. That makes it more likely that those who disagree with you will lash out. So, there is that to deal with.

## ANDREW ROBINSON

Celebrity is a two-edged sword that sometimes brings riches and fame to the celebrity, but also can bring difficulty and pain. No story I've seen illustrates this point better than the stories I have both heard from and also read by my good friend Andrew Robinson. When *DS9* first aired, the most compelling character for me by far on this show was Garak, the Cardassian Tailor. Garak is a complex character in a Cardassian mask, and wearing that mask was an exercise of patience and tolerance (as were wearing the masks for all of my actor friends in *Star Trek*). By the time Andy was cast for *Star Trek*, he was already a well-known face from American cinema and television. His very first iconic role in the film *Dirty Harry*, also starring Clint Eastwood, was for Andy a life changing experience that sent him in an entirely new direction, both in life and in his career. Andy portrayed the evil serial Scorpio killer in that film and at the time his agent told him that based on his performance in this film, he was going to be a big star. Andy recounts (Robinson, 2015):

> I readily capitulated to this sudden and warm attention from honey-tongued people, and I didn't show much character as I dumped my energetic and faithful New York agent, Billy Barnes, and went with the L.A. office of William Morris. The prospect of becoming a star was like finding a miracle cure to all my ailments. . . . I changed agents and behaved as if I had suddenly become an important person.
>
> (p. 255)

He got a second prominent role in *Charley Varrick*, co-starring with Walter Matthau. "This was going to be my life now and I plastered over my insecurity with the arrogance of someone who has made it" (p. 255). This film was a great experience, but what followed was a sequence of frustrating missteps and the realization ultimately that he had been typecast as an evil bad guy. Roles outside of that stereotype were elusive, so much so that he ultimately left acting for a time. He had a number of experiences where, having been recognized for his role as Scorpio in *Dirty Harry*, people would cross the street to avoid him or would come right up to him and say that he was the stuff of their nightmares. It was a disheartening time to say the least.

After a period where he pursued other things and reflected on all that had happened, he returned to acting with a renewed sense of who he was as an actor. He went on to pursue a number of exciting roles including *Liberace* in the made for television movie of his life. *Star Trek* came later after having done years of television and film, as well as live theater. Andy is also an accomplished director, having won the Los Angeles Drama Critics' Circle award for directing at the Matrix Theater in Hollywood. But it is still the case that he is recognized for *Dirty Harry* as often as for the many roles he has played since.

At the end of his book, he recounts, "learning how to act well is as demanding as living a conscious and truthful life" (p. 280). Andy began a new career as a college professor in the Master of Fine Arts program at University of Southern California several years after *DS9* ended. Part of finding his way back after the difficult years after *Dirty Harry* has been to teach young people about the craft of acting, both at USC and years earlier in workshops he developed for teens at summer camps. He talks frequently in his book about the importance of maintaining a "beginner's mind" in his work as an actor. Conveying what that means to his students has become an important part of his life and career.

Looking back at the earlier discussion in the chapter on values, except for a brief detour into a quest for celebrity recognition, clearly lifelong values for Andy are self-direction, stimulation, benevolence, and universalism. He was among the most committed of the *DS9* actors to the charity work that we did as he has had a lifelong passion for *Save the Children* (one of the charities for whom we raised money) for many years.

## CONCLUSIONS

Several themes emerge from the material offered by these various actors. What stands out first is that fame definitely happens on many different levels. Siddig refers to himself as "mid ranked I suppose," while Rene calls himself a "character" actor and Aron a "working actor." Armin is reluctant to embrace the term "celebrity" at all, admitting to being a "public figure." Andy, in his autobiography, talks about being in the "Giant People's Club," something he was assured of having attained (by his agent) after *Dirty Harry*, and was disappointed when the promised roles failed to appear after the first two big movies.

Having been "typecast" after *Star Trek*, in the case of Chase, Armin, and Siddig, and after *Dirty Harry* for Andy was a career problem, one that other actors in the *Star Trek* world have also recounted in their talks at the many conventions I have attended. Siddig pursued a film career after *DS9* ended. He accepted a role on the film *TheVertical Limit*, which he told me he got in spite of *Star Trek* rather than because of it, uncertain as to if he'd get another chance to do a major film if he didn't take the opportunity. The lesson here is that if you do most of your work in one genre, getting other work becomes progressively more difficult. A recent interview with Hugh Jackman had him recounting that in his early career in Australia, he had done quite a few musicals but had to hold off on doing them because it was making it difficult to get straight acting work. He has recently returned to musicals now after having had success as a big movie star, but for a time he didn't dare do them (www.youtube.com/watch?v=UEt5Jjkjl2w).

Several actors mentioned that it was annoying for others to assume that they were wealthy or part of a "Hollywood Elite" simply for having appeared on national television. All those interviewed work hard at their craft, and are committed to quality acting, whether on stage or screen. Siddig himself described the Hollywood stereotype when he said, "I found out that you can be a Hollywood actor and not be what I used to think of as a Hollywood actor. . . . I would think of someone who is self-aggrandizing, someone who lived for the publicity coup." This appears to be the stereotype that many people hold when thinking about celebrities, Hollywood celebrities in particular. None of the celebrities, interviewed here or others that I know, meet that stereotype. It is necessary to penetrate the upper echelons of celebrity before even some of the people live up to that stereotype. Rene, when he talked to me about Baryshnikov, was quick to assure me that he was a humble and very nice guy, clearly feeling the need to do damage control against the prevailing stereotype of superstar celebrities.

We sometimes react to the familiarity of the person on television as if they are someone we really know in our day-to-day lives, and it is hard to remember that they don't know us as we know them. Rene's experience in airports where people see him and think they must know each other is a reflection of that. Or Siddig's comment that "once someone knows me from the screen, they treat me as a friend." And later that celebrities "will never make friends the way ordinary people do." Being known from film and television is a complicating factor in a celebrity's life.

A similar point is that audience members have a difficult time realizing the difference between the actor and his or her character. Siddig recounted that people write to him as if he were a real doctor instead of playing one on television. A similar problem for celebrities in pursuing relationships is the inability to be perceived as oneself. Ava Gardner recounted:

> Rita Hayworth once said the problem with her life was that the men in it fell in love with Gilda, her most glamorous role, and woke up the next morning with her. That's a sentiment I can fully identify with. I've always felt a prisoner of my image, felt that people preferred the myths and didn't want to hear about the real me at all.
>
> (Gardner, 1990, p. 114)

That celebrities can be fans themselves is brought into sharp relief with Armin's experience meeting Stephen Hawking. Interviews given by Josh Groban where he recounted getting to work with the idols of his childhood, people like Paul Simon and John Williams, echo the same theme, that the people we "meet" through media, and who have iconic status in our culture affect us all.

Arthur Miller's (2013) words echo in my mind "that such an order of recognition imprints its touch of arrogance" (p. 193). It seems that some who achieve fame have to work very hard at not letting it go to their heads (as in Andy's struggle just after *Dirty Harry*). However, what I have experienced is that it is those around the big stars, who work for them and "protect" them from the public, who are much more likely to think of themselves with an inflated sense of importance. It was not Michael Jackson (with whom I interacted a number of times) who came off as arrogant, but rather most of those who worked for him who thought they were better than everyone else, as if their association with Jackson, their employment by him, made them important. They also worked very hard to protect their status in the sphere of his celebrity by working very hard to keep everyone else away. Many who work for a big superstar like Jackson are about denying access to "their" star. I shared my graduate thesis on Michael Jackson fans with him and with his staff. Jackson himself showed great interest in my findings, asking many questions about various things. Those just under him, the gatekeepers, were sure I was after their jobs, or that I was there to somehow reveal the ways that they took advantage of fans (which happened frequently in the case of that fandom, I discovered). It was inconceivable to them that I would just share my work . . . to share my work.

It reveals something to me about "show business" to know that everyone who worked for Jackson who met me during those years (1989 to 1992) was trying to find out "my angle." What was I after? Thinking about values, it did not seem to be conceivable to any of them, with one exception, that my values of achievement coupled with benevolence and universalism were what were at work. I was trying to achieve advanced degrees, and if I could help someone else in the process, why not? One of the many who worked for Jackson who seemed to "get" that and responded to me with kindness and friendliness was Bill Bray, Jackson's chief of security, and we had many meetings to discuss the work I was doing and to try and explore insights into what the motivation was behind fandom, the topic of my thesis and dissertation.

Negative fame of the kind experienced by Andy Robinson after *Dirty Harry* is not something with which I have had much experience or about which I have seen too much written. Anyone who has played a role that caused people to be fearful or insecure would potentially be the recipient of that kind of negative attention. It's an area in social science that could use a great deal more exploration.

In summary, being a superstar celebrity seems to make life very difficult. Privacy is sacrificed, and some members of the public invade the space of people they don't know at all, because media create the illusion of intimacy. Arthur Miller (2013), husband of Marilyn Monroe, captures very well the extreme difficulty of living such a life:

> A movie star of Marilyn's magnitude is obviously no longer human, but what she is instead is hard to define without calling up the supernatural; she is a form of longing in the public's imagination, and in that sense godlike.
>
> (p. 428)

Speaking of her fan mail he recounted a host of really odd things she would receive, from containers of feces to offers to put her out of her misery, observing that,

> something like fifteen percent (of the letter writers) were quite insane. . . . Marilyn rarely had the peace of mind to look at the bags of letters (p. 428). Going out with Marilyn . . . was a major logistical operation.
>
> (p. 434)

As her life became more and more challenged by her fame, he observed, "She was Marilyn Monroe and that was what was killing her" (p. 483). In 1962, she succumbed to an overdose of barbiturates, an early end to a life made tragic by her celebrity. While not all big stars have such an ending, fame of this magnitude certainly seems to put one at risk.

In contrast, celebrities like the ones interviewed here seem to have achieved a level of fame where the positive aspects of that life more than outweigh negative aspects.

# 5

## CELEBRITIES AND THEIR FANS

Celebrity is an easy thing to study at a distance because its influence is everywhere, but one should not take for granted the extent of cultural influence that celebrities exert (Couldry, 2004; Driessens, 2013). It has always been easy for academics to sit in the "Ivory Tower" and theorize about such things. One of the pluses of 30 years of fieldwork in fan studies is that I do not just have to theorize about the influence of celebrities. I have seen it personally and in many situations. Later in this chapter is a recap of the experiences I have had doing fieldwork in fan studies.

### PARASOCIAL RELATIONSHIPS (PSR)

There has been a fair amount of misunderstanding about this term, parasocial. The official definition means that the relationship is non-reciprocated or one-way. I know the celebrity, but he or she does not know me. In the case of parasocial interaction (PSI), I interact without someone there to respond to me, the classic example is watching a scary movie and saying, "No . . . Don't go in there! Don't do that," although we know full well that the characters can't hear us and that what we say will have no effect on their behavior. Or we yell at the sports figure on the television when she or he misses a play, or does well. We react to them even though we know they can't hear us.

Does "parasocial" in any way infer pathology? Many experts in parasocial research would easily say no, and the conversations I have had with scholars who pathologize parasocial are usually from disciplines other than mass communication. Parasocial scholar Riva Tukachinsky, a communication professor, has insisted to me that it is not necessary to say "parasocial" is normal because it so clearly is in the realm of normal behavior.

I agree with this and have been baffled as to where this origin of an association between parasocial and any kind of "abnormality" might have originated. Virtually everyone interacts in a parasocial way with media, and most of us carry the feelings we have for those characters and actors we see in media beyond the actual viewing of media (the PSR).

One possibility involves a very specific form of PSR, the "celebrity worshipper," a concept put forth by Lynn McCutcheon, John Maltby, and others and measured using the Celebrity Attitude Scale (CAS). Work on the CAS (McCutcheon, Maltby, Houran, & Ashe, 2004) found that for general population samples, 3–5% gave "borderline-pathological" responses. "If my favorite celebrity asked me to do something illegal, I would do it," was the kind of item to which this small percentage of participants responded positively. Next, 20% were high on the "intense personal" scale of the CAS, taken from community and student samples (sample item: My favorite celebrity is my soul mate and if he or she were to die, I wouldn't want to live). Clearly celebrity worship is alive and well today in the 21st century.

For the fans I had met in my research, my sense was that the percentages would not be any higher, if that high. In 2008–9, I gave the CAS to samples of Josh Groban fans and Star Trek fans. Each group showed the highest level of commitment to their favorite celebrities, but the levels of celebrity worship measured were the same as the general populations samples or less (with only 15% of the Star Trek fans in the "intense personal" category). My belief that among organized fan groups, celebrity worship was not the norm was reinforced by this study (Stever, 2011b).

Celebrity worship having a pathological extreme comes down to a "which comes first, the chicken or the egg" kind of question. Do mentally ill people develop pathological celebrity worship, or does pathological celebrity worship cause a person to become mentally ill? Or could both things come into play? Clearly a great deal more research would need to be done to definitively answer these questions.

## BEGINNING MY FAN STUDIES

In 1988, as a graduate student, I had ideas about what "superstar mania" might look like . . . and went to my first Michael Jackson concert to test those ideas. I thought this was principally an adolescent phenomenon and that there would be a lot of frenzied, crazy behavior. What would a typical fan look like? Within hours at my first show, it was clear that my preconceived ideas were wrong. Jackson was 31 years old, and his fans clustered around his age, with a large percentage of them being within five years of his age, so 26 to 36 . . . not adolescents at all. Entering the arena for the first time, couples were dressed up for date night, looking nice and behaving normally. Then a television news camera came around the arena looking for fans to interview, and the fans went a bit crazy. They were trying to get in front of the camera and when they were, they would scream and carry on, behaving like the typical fans seen on television with Elvis or The Beatles.

Presumably, those fans had seen the same frenzied behavior on television that I had seen, and they knew how they were "supposed to act." They followed the script and responded on cue to the cameras. As soon as the camera crew had passed on, the fans reverted to their normal conversations and calm behavior. I had to reexamine and adjust all of my assumptions and plans for my study. I renewed my commitment to fieldwork where I could observe first-hand behavior. During the Michael Jackson shows (and indeed the subsequent shows for Madonna, Janet Jackson, and others) there was dancing and singing along, but little hysteria or screaming.

In 1992, at a Michael Jackson show at Wembley Stadium in London, cameras recorded fans overcome and fainting. On that day (July 31), fans had been standing out on the field in more than 80 degrees Fahrenheit for five or more hours. They were being treated for dehydration and heat-related illness. None of that information came through on the video depictions of these events. This is not to say that fans are never overcome with emotion in the presence of their favorite celebrity, but creating a frenzy or getting a crowd to react emotionally had as much to do with media presence and crowd mismanagement as it did genuine emotions being expressed by fans.

In total, I attended 15 Michael Jackson concerts, two in Maryland, three at Irvine Meadows, five at the Los Angeles Sports Arena, and five in the United Kingdom (three in London, one in Cardiff, and one in Leeds). I also went to awards shows where Jackson appeared, a press conference, a music video taping in a small airport hangar, and two Michaelfests organized by a fan-run fan club, one in 1989 and one in 1990.

Adrian Grant was a 19-year-old fan who published Off The Wall, a British magazine and easily the best Jackson-based publication of the time. Michael Jackson agreed, and Adrian was given access to Neverland Ranch (Jackson's home) and wrote a profile for his magazine, the only journalist ever allowed that access. I did some reporting for Adrian (thus the press conference for the magazine) and stayed in the homes of magazine staff during my three-week trip to England in 1992. I also stayed with journalism professor John Powner and his family who lived in Stoke-on-Trent; he was doing research on the Jackson fandom. We exchanged data and spent hours discussing findings. I had access to his notes and he to mine. During my four-year study of this fan group, I networked among a core of participants on two continents and for a time observed some of the most ardent fan behavior in my 30 years of study. Grant went on to create the hit London West End stage show, Thriller – Live.

During that same time, I attended two Beatlefests and met with a dedicated group of fans not only of The Beatles but particularly of Paul McCartney's solo career. I attended the Arizona State stadium show in

1990, surveying a sample of 70,000 fans who were there. Add to this six Madonna shows on her 1990 *Blonde Ambition* tour and six shows on the Janet Jackson *Rhythm Nation* tour in 1989. Fan networks of Bruce Springsteen, Prince, George Michael, as well as Madonna filled out surveys by mail, approximately 70 from each group. Phenomenally, I got back every single one of the questionnaire sets that I mailed out, about 300 of them. To say fans were interested in what I was trying to discover would be an understatement. The questionnaires sent out included the Celebrity Appeal Questionnaire, an instrument I developed for this research (Stever, 1991b, 2008). Also included was the Myers Briggs Type Indicator, a personality questionnaire discussed later in this chapter.

All of these prime examples of superstar mania involved prominent celebrities of international renown. The largest percentage of fans whom I met were thoughtful and reasonable. When they found out about my research, they were eager to understand not only their own interest but also the interests of others.

## MOVING ON TO OTHER GROUPS OF FANS

My fieldwork in science fiction fandom spanned from 1991 to approximately 2010 and in that time I attended hundreds of conventions and other fan events. I had the privilege of getting to know the celebrities interviewed in Chapter 4. I assisted in autograph lines for many *Star Trek* actors, as well as for John Rhys Davies (*Lord of the Rings*). I have observed fans meeting Josh Groban at CD signings, backstage meet and greets, Broadway stage door meetings, and after concert informal autograph sessions, also observing photo ops with William Shatner, Leonard Nimoy, Scott Bakula, Karl Urban, and various other actors, and Jake Gyllenhaal autographing for fans after three Broadway shows. I saw Michael Jackson meeting mostly other celebrities at a cocktail party following a press conference in 1990, as well as before concerts. I have been part of a studio audience for shows like *Ellen, Frazier, Becker, Live! with Kelly* (Ripa), *Jimmy Kimmel Live!*, and various awards shows (MTV, the Grammys, etc.), all places where fans obtained photos with and autographs from celebrities. While I have read a great deal about fan/celebrity interactions, influence, and identification, I have learned almost as much (or maybe more) through in-person, real-life encounters.

## ACCESS TO CELEBRITIES

We defined celebrities of the 20th century by their remoteness, our lack of access to them, and the mystique that "handlers" created around them by keeping the public away. By the end of the 20th century and into the 21st, stars were more and more speaking for themselves, writing their own agendas, and choosing to have a more direct relationship with audiences. This is not to say that ALL celebrities are doing this, but rather that such a significant number of them are doing so that the nature of the relationship (or at least potential relationship) between stars and audiences is changed forever. In my article, "Meeting Josh Groban (Again)" (2016a), I made the case that by creating direct lines of communication with fans and not only being known more directly by fans and also knowing more fans personally, the nature of fan/celebrity interaction is fundamentally changed for the celebrities who choose to take this path. The rise of social media played a big part in this shift. Large media conventions also play a part.

For example, ComiCons around the country feature A-list celebrities (those who are the biggest of stars with the largest of salaries). At such events, audience members have a chance to speak directly with these stars, something that almost never happened earlier in the 20th century, although soap opera stars possibly led the way in this area by meeting fans at conventions (Harrington, 2010). A recent ComiCon in San Diego featured Johnny Galicki and Kelly Cuoco of *The Big Bang Theory*, two of the highest paid actors on television on one of the most popular television shows of this decade. In a video of the show's panel (accessible on cbs.com), audience members are shown interacting personally with these big name actors. In a previous year, I saw similar interactions with Halle Berry and Angelina Jolie at the 2004 ComiCon. It should be noted that in its early years beginning in 1970, ComiCon, San Diego was much more focused on comic books but as it evolved, more and more "stars" appeared there until in the 1990s the guest lists contain names like William Shatner and Francis Ford Coppola. Most recently, a shift to promoting television shows has happened such that the television stars now outnumber the comic book people. The attendance began in 1970 at 145 people, but now yearly attendance tops 150,000 (https://en.wikipedia.org/wiki/San_Diego_Comic-Con).

## MEETING YOUR FAVORITE CELEBRITY

Why can meeting a celebrity in person be such a jarring experience? While we encounter them in the media on a daily basis, meeting celebrities in person is a comparatively rare occurrence. The first time I saw Michael Jackson in person on stage, I remember having trouble processing the fact that he was real and right in front of me. Iconic media figures in particular are processed for symbolic value rather than as human beings.

In 1993, I met and eventually became friends with *Star Trek* actor Alexander Siddig, Dr. Bashir on *Deep Space Nine* (DS9). Right after I had met him for the first time, I watched DS9 and had a hard time connecting the character on the show with the person I was getting to know on a real and human level. In a similar way to that first Jackson encounter, it had a feeling of unreality about it. The sense of the real/unreal dichotomy persisted for some time. I have known him quite well now for 25 years, and I am not sure I can pinpoint when that sense of unreality faded for me, but it did and was less true for each of the subsequent actors that I came to know. Then there was a day where I was on the set of DS9 and in walked James Darren who played Vic Fontaine but is better known for his work on *TJ Hooker*, *Gidget*, and *The Time Tunnel*. At that point, I was about as immune to being "star struck" as I could be and yet in an instant, I was my 15-year-old self again and that 15-year-old girl had a crush on James Darren during his years on *The Time Tunnel*. The encounter rendered me almost speechless, but I managed to stutter out a hello.

I share this experience because it highlights the special status that media figures have in our lives when we have developed a significant sense of connection with them or with their characters. Because I "knew" Darren as a teen, I reacted differently to him based on the awe that was a holdover from my adolescence. Actors are just people doing a job, but my adolescent fantasies about the character were still with me . . . in a very real sense, I "knew" him. Such is the essence of a parasocial relationship (PSR), also referred to as "intimacy at a distance." Such PSRs have a particularly important place in adolescent development, as they become imagined romantic relationships that are practice for future real ones.

## MEETING CELEBRITIES

Given that parasocial is defined as "one way knowing" that is not reciprocated, two conversations about meeting celebrities are necessary. One is about fans who personally know and are known by a celebrity, and a different one is about fans who have never had access and thus have only interacted with the celebrity in their imaginations (the PSR). While it is possible for either kind of interaction to have an element of dysfunction or pathology, in my 30 years of experience networking within fan communities, this has been the exception rather than the rule. As discussed above, it makes no more sense to say either fan/celebrity relationships or PSRs are pathological because they have the potential to be, than it would be to say all social relationships are pathological simply because they have that potential.

Noted author in fan studies Matt Hills (2016) stated that "fans are required to respect the celebrity's privacy" (p. 466) and stick to a limited range of conversations. Other scholars have made similar allegations, for example, Marwick and boyd (2011) who said that autograph signings and other opportunities to meet celebrities are "highly managed and limited in scope" (p. 149). I have yet to see any actual research evidence that this is true.

In fact, this is no more necessarily true than it would be in any other social situation. A good percentage of fan/celebrity encounters are not pre-staged. In my 2016 article on celebrities as friendly acquaintances, I argue that much more is taken away from fan/celebrity meetings than just photos and autographs. Twitter (Stever & Lawson, 2013) has also enhanced the ability of interested celebrities to respond personally to fans who are known to that celebrity (see Rene Auberjonois' comments in Chapter 4). After nine years of following Josh Groban on Twitter, it is clear that he responds individually to fans he knows. An important question is "When does the PSR cross over into the social?" Additionally, while access to celebrities can be big business as described by Ferris and Harris (2011), celebrities can easily circumvent those mechanisms if they so choose, as I frequently observed in both Star Trek and Josh Groban fandoms. Private room parties with well-known fans were the norm for many of the DS9 actors, and Josh Groban would frequently come out after concerts or Broadway shows to chat with fans informally. Indeed, even Michael Jackson had a small subset of fans with whom he interacted personally at his own initiative.

The significance of fan/celebrity relationships in the scope of a lifetime is meaningful for many individuals. A lifetime relationship with a famous person can have a primary impact on identity and other aspects of social development.

As Hills (2016) pointed out, all social relationships have an element of imagination linked to them. In this sense, the PSR is not unique. Contrary to what some have theorized (Jenson, 1992), PSRs are often not something we have in order to make up for a lack in our lives, particularly when PSR and fan activity take place in the context of a social community. The fan in isolation behaves very differently to the fan as a part of a community. Community serves as a reality check for things like "no one loves X as much as I do." It is easy to maintain that illusion when one doesn't know any other fans. It is also necessary to distinguish love of a person from love of their work.

As a person who has participated multiple times in all the forms of "pre-staged" fan/celebrity encounters including conventions, in-store promotions, or charity events (Hills, 2016) the assumption that these encounters are scripted in some way is a false one. While they can be rushed, they aren't always. A lot of it has to do with the motivation of the celebrity. In 1994, Siddig contacted his newly formed *Star Trek* fan club, frustrated with the impersonal nature of convention autograph lines. He wanted a more relaxed and personal chance to meet fans and get to know them and what they thought of the show (see his discussion in Chapter 4). From this request was born "Lunch with the Doctor," an event that was held in various forms annually from 1994 to 2003 where attendance ranged from 65 to 150 fans. In 1998, at the San Diego event, Siddig spent an average of nearly five minutes with each of 115 fans, chatting, posing, and autographing (yes, that was a total of over nine hours throughout the day). With annual opportunities of this kind, in addition to other encounters at events like conventions, a rather sizeable subset of his fans came to know him quite well. A long list of *DS9* actors participated in such events including Nana Visitor, Rene Auberjonois, Andrew Robinson, Armin Shimerman, Chase Masterson, Aron Eisenberg, Max Grodenchik, JG Hertzler, the already mentioned Siddig, and others. Additionally the *Star Trek Voyager* fan clubs hosted similar events, and those fans came to know their actors as well. Patrick Stewart (Picard of *Next Generation*), William Shatner (Captain Kirk of the original series), and actors from the other *Star Trek* shows also had opportunities where fans were able to interact personally and get to know their favorites.

Among commercial events, Creation Entertainment (run by long-time *Star Trek* fans Adam Malin and Gary Berman) has started offering the "Meet and Greet" where, for a fee, four to five fans can visit with a given actor for half an hour in a private room. I have observed similar opportunities for Josh Groban fans and know from fan reports that such opportunities are not isolated or unique. I have dialogued with fans of Russell Crowe, Nathan Fillian, Jeri Ryan, Craig Parker, Michael Crawford, and others, enough so that I am convinced that the opportunity to have a personal, unscripted conversation with a favorite celebrity is not an aberration.

As Hills (2016) and Ferris and Harris (2011) describe fan celebrity interactions, one major type seems to be left out of their classification schema. They enumerate the pre-staged encounter, usually commercial; the fan-staged encounter, which frankly sounds something akin to stalking; and the un-staged or random encounter. However, sometimes celebrities negotiate agreed upon or mutually understood situations where fans have learned they can talk to their favorite celebrities. These don't really fit the "commercial" category, but they also are not un-staged or random. They certainly are not fan-staged in the sense that the fan has "hunted down" the celebrity in order to have the encounter, an idea that most fans I've interviewed find to be creepy. Rather, these are mutually agreed upon situations where celebrities make themselves available rather consistently and fans, most often members of a community where such knowledge is shared, know they can meet and talk to the artist. Most Broadway stars, for example, come out after shows and talk to fans, pose for selfies, and sign autographs. I observed that even A-list movie stars, like already mentioned Jake Gyllenhaal, would do this.

## PERSONAL EXAMPLES

My friend Rose was a very special person. I met her during my *Star Trek* fan research, and in 2003, we lost her to colon cancer. Rose was a friend that I mainly saw at *Star Trek* conventions and other fan events. Rose went to enough fan events that her favorite *Star Trek* celebrities knew her by name. She was engaging and friendly and collected LOTS of autographs. She had all of the *Star Trek* collector's plates (the ones offered by Franklin Mint), and she had every one of them autographed. To say being a *Star Trek* fan was an important part of her identity would have been an understatement.

Beginning in 1994, the DS9 actors and later the *Voyager* actors held the above mentioned yearly charity events that were small and personal, and Rose attended them all. In August of 2003, we attended our last convention together, and a Creation Entertainment employee who found out Rose was terminal and attending her last convention kindly gave her a VIP pass, which got us backstage to talk more easily to some of the actors with whom she had become friends. Armin Shimerman and Kitty Swink (DS9 actors married to one another) were particularly good friends of Rose's, and Kitty is a cancer survivor. I can still see them sitting there with Rose, tears in their eyes, talking with her one last time about what was going on, knowing that the end was near. Alexander Siddig, Robert Picardo . . . several of the actors spent time with her at this convention, knowing that they were saying good-bye.

Another fan who became friends with a celebrity was a woman known in the Josh Groban fandom as "Michigan Connie." Connie had worked very hard on Josh's charity foundation along with fan and close friend Val Sooky. Together with other fans, they had formed Grobanites for Charity (GFC), the fan-run arm of the Josh Groban Foundation. GFC worked tirelessly starting in 2003 to raise money for Josh's charity causes, surpassing the $1 million mark by 2010. I never met Connie as I met the fan group about five months after she had passed away following her battle with cancer. Nevertheless, I was at the Detroit concert in 2007 where Josh Groban dedicated a song to her during the concert and had a special greeting backstage for her daughters who had come that night.

Over 30 years, I have participated in numerous and varied fan groups as part of my research. There would be no reason to suspect that what I encountered in these groups with celebrities as varied as Michael Jackson, Josh Groban, William Shatner, and many others was unique or unusual. Fans and celebrities meet, they exchange meaningful conversations, sometimes they become known quite well to one another, even if the meetings are infrequent, and while yes some fan meetings are controlled and managed, many more are not.

## SIMILARITY/HOMOPHILY

Much has been said on the subject of how celebrities enhance the development of identity through their presence as role models. Aspirational figures are people who, by their very presence in our lives, give us goals to reach for and ways that we can better ourselves.

One of the best predictors of whether or not a viewer will follow a celebrity is similarity, also referred to in the academic literature as homophily. There are a number of research studies supporting the idea that we tend to become followers of celebrities whom we most perceive to be like us in some significant way. Remember that it is the perception rather than the reality that is important.

For my master's thesis back in the late 1980s, I asked participants to take the Myers Briggs Type Indicator (MBTI), which measures personality qualities such as introversion and extroversion or sensing perception vs. intuitive perception (for a discussion of Jungian personality see Myers & Myers, 2010). The scales in the MBTI render a four-letter personality type. After taking this questionnaire, the fan was asked to fill it out again the way he or she thought the favorite celebrity would answer. This is a measure of perceived rather than actual personality, but the consistent finding was that fans agreed almost 100% about what personality their favorite star had, and the overall fan personality type matched the star's personality at a rate far higher than what could be attributable by chance.

An example will make this clearer. In the general population in the United States, about 1 in 4 persons is Introverted, and a further 1 in 4 is the Intuitive personality type. This means that 1 in 16 people is both Introverted and Intuitive. Of 100 sampled Michael Jackson fans, 60% were Introverted Intuitive and all agreed that this was his personality type. Of 100 sampled Prince fans, 65% were Introverted Intuitive, again with 100% agreement among those same fans that this was his type. Sampled fans were behaviorally identified as being serious followers of the artist. There are a great deal more data of this type in my two publications on this subject (Stever, 1991a, 1995).

A later study (McCarley & Escoto, 2003) tried to replicate my finding, but it used a sample of college students rather than behaviorally identified fans. The selection of subjects for the study was exactly the reason why they got no connection between favorite celebrity and personality type. If you take a random normative sample of college students and ask them to identify their favorite celebrity, this presumes that they all have a favorite celebrity for whom they feel some investment, or to whom they feel a commitment. However, only a subset of those students would meet the criteria for "behaviorally identified fan." Those criteria included those who had extensive

memorabilia collections, joined fan clubs, traveled to multiple concerts, or participated in pen pal lists for their favorite celebrity. Most
participants in my study met more than one of these criteria. The
celebrity was someone they had integrated into their daily lives and
followed with loyalty and commitment. It was at this level of fandom
that the similarity was found. Clearly, at the initiation phase of an
interest in a celebrity, this similarity is not so pronounced, or indeed
the self-selection process that resulted in the personality type being
the same had not yet taken place. In the late 1980s, many people
would have said (indeed, did say), "I am a Michael Jackson fan," as
Jackson had sold over 50 million copies of his album *Thriller* in the US
alone. However, that level of interest would not have qualified them
for my study.

The same study was conducted on a sample of *Star Trek* fans who
identified an actor as a favorite from among the *Star Trek* actors (samples were taken for fans of Nana Visitor and Siddig, from DS9). This
same high selection of introverted intuitive fans was found.

However, one might speculate that there was something about
being an introverted intuitive that attracted people to fandoms in
general. That was something I could not rule out as every artist whose
fans were sampled was deemed an introvert and an intuitive by the
fans, not surprising given that the normative samples for MBTI for
artists also show a trend towards both introversion and intuition.
A sample of fans of a celebrity perceived to be an extrovert would
have been helpful, but after defending my master's thesis, my research
took different directions.

A number of other studies have found a correlation between celebrities and their followers based on perceived similarities. Other studies have not supported this finding (like the one referred to above),
suggesting that it takes commitment to a favorite celebrity before this
is observed.

While I did some survey research with good samples taken (see
my published articles for descriptions of how sampling was done), a
good deal of the research has been qualitative, based on observational
field notes, interviews transcribed and coded, written documents

analyzed, and so forth. Qualitative work is harder to generalize to other samples. It should also be noted that all of the fan groups within which I participated had mostly positive role models and good people who were the objects of fan interest. If I had looked at celebrities deemed to be "negative" influences (just figuring out how to define that would be a challenge), there could have been some different findings. This is the nature of social science research in the qualitative realm.

# 6

---

# DE-MASSIFICATION OF MEDIA AND THE BIRTH OF SOCIAL MEDIA

As already discussed in Chapter 2, Toffler identified the 1980s as the beginnings of the de-massification of media, meaning we went from large audiences watching a very few channels, to smaller audiences choosing from hundreds of channels, or a handful of available magazines to thousands. Where media choices had been limited, now there were many. This impacted celebrity as already noted by making it harder to reach the same mass audience that the mid-20th-century superstars like Elvis Presley, The Beatles, and Michael Jackson were able to reach.

The media explosion was followed by the introduction of the personal computer, affordable for the masses by the 1980s. Then in the 1990s, the Internet, which up until that point had been for an elite and technically savvy population, widened such that anyone who owned a personal computer and a modem could get online.

Media ceased to be the "one size fits all" model that was prominent earlier in the 20th century. In that era, a great deal of power was held by a very few individuals. Media power was centralized, and media were used to get out the message that people in power wanted to have disseminated. This model of mass media dominated the 19th and 20th centuries until, starting in the 1980s, the de-centralization of media began.

## THE BIRTH OF SOCIAL MEDIA

Beginning in the first decade of the 21st century, social media in various forms exploded onto the World Wide Web or Internet, and various social media sites have become hugely influential as a result.

The advent of the Internet and the birth of social media expanded the number of niche markets, each with its own micro-celebrities. Micro-celebrity is a term coined by Senft (2008) in her book about "Camgirls." These were young women who broadcast their personal lives to audience subscribers. Micro-celebrity describes someone who has a fan base in a single medium such as a YouTube channel, a blog, a website, or a social media page. The first "Camgirl," "Jennicam," began broadcasting in 1996, ending in 2004. Senft's book gives a detailed history of Camgirls including her own venture into being a Camgirl herself, although her broadcast was part of her research into the phenomenon. From her work comes an understanding of the dynamic between Camgirls and their audiences.

Micro-celebrities have overlapped into the world of mainstream media. Examples include Hayes Grier, a YouTube star who appeared on season 21 of *Dancing with the Stars*, as did YouTube fashion blogger Bethany Mota in season 19. CBS news (November 9, 2015) posted the article "10 YouTube Stars You Need to Know," including Michael Stevens of VSauce, an online science program. YouTube streams varied topics where people create and potentially later become known for their videos. Micro-celebrities known as "Influencers" first appeared in Singapore in 2005 and included young women bloggers using their online presence to self-brand and share fashion and makeup advice. This is an industry-related term recognizing their marketing potential (Abidin, 2017). Influencers prefer the term "followers" to fans (Abidin, 2015) thinking that it reduces the distance between the SMI (Social Media Influencer) and the follower. The self-perception is that they are just like anyone else. Social media is ever expanding with newer forms like Snapchat and Instagram being added to the mix (Giles, 2018).

As social media grew in prominence, this venue for micro-celebrities and their followers was soon also adopted by mainstream celebrities (Marwick & boyd, 2011).

## FAME AND THE PURSUIT OF FAME AND CELEBRITY

One of the big draws of social media is the prospect on the part of the user of realizing some level of fame, celebrity, or recognition, at least in one's own corner of the world. Greenwood (2013) found that a desire for visibility was the best predictor of frequent social media use among those surveyed, particularly with respect to celebrity-oriented social media use (following celebrities or responding to their posts).

Because our society emphasizes material and economic rewards as an expected outcome of fame, fame seeking is a logical pursuit for those who want to be counted among the "rich and famous" (Holmes & Redmond, 2012). Some narratives have emphasized the negative aspects of celebrity and fame, seeing this as a damaging and negative force in society. While this can be true, and we have explored some of those negative aspects of celebrity (see Chapter 4), the potentially positive aspects of celebrity are of interest as well.

That a pursuit of fame and celebrity is the result of things that are lacking in individual lives seems a reasonable conclusion and one that has been pursued by many writers. Studies have identified social inclusion as a fundamental need (Baumeister & Leary, 1995). Additional studies have linked a desire for fame with this need for inclusion, and recent research (Pinker, 2015) has found that social contact and inclusion is the best predictor of long life. Additionally, if you feel that your death is imminent, your desire for fame and admiration for fame increases (Greenberg, Kosloff, Solomon, Cohen, & Landau, 2010). Greenwood, Long, and Dal Cin (2013) found that not only the need to belong but also narcissism were factors that increased a person's desire for fame.

To what extent loneliness is the catalyst for the pursuit of both parasocial (non-reciprocated) relationships with media figures and also fan/celebrity interaction in the real world is a question that has been met with mixed findings. This question is particularly relevant as we consider social media, the place where fans have some success in interacting with a wide variety of their favorite celebrities.

What other psychological factors have been identified as correlating with a desire for fame? Maltby et al. (2008) explored nine correlates for fame: The first six were the most important in what was called an "implicit theory of fame," referring to the underlying beliefs people have for why they think others seek fame. These were ambition, meaning derived through comparison with others, psychological vulnerability, attention seeking, conceitedness, and a desire for social access. Three other factors that did not have as strong an influence were altruism, confidence, and glamor. A second study, reported in the same article, involving evaluation of fictional cases and their perceived desire for fame, reinforced the first six factors plus glamor as being robust predictors of others' desire for fame.

There is no clear evidence for exactly how many people really desire fame. While Greenberg et al. (2010) felt that "most people in the USA probably long to be famous, or at least did so as children" (p. 6), no evidence was given to support that claim. A 2006 Pew Research Center survey (Kohut et al., 2006) found that a majority of 18- to 25-year-olds reported fame and fortune as their generation's most valued life goals. But this may not be consistent with a finding reported by Maltby et al. (2008) that "according to the UK's Learning and Skills Council (in Maltby et al., 2008), 16 per cent of 16–19 year olds presently believe they are going to become famous, and 11 per cent are prepared to abandon formal education in pursuit of that goal" (Maltby et al., 2008, p. 3; Turner, 2010). Perhaps the contrast is between a desire to be famous and the actual belief that this will happen?

The desire for fame or to be connected with the famous seems like one explanation for the explosion of social media in our culture.

## REALITY TV VS. SOCIAL MEDIA

When talking about celebrities who seem to have being "rich and famous" as their end goal, the most cited example has been the

Kardashians, stars of their own reality television show. So much has been said about this family of celebrities that I am reluctant to say much more, except to observe that this category of celebrity is not new as explained with the example of Oscar Wilde in Chapter 3. Famous people most often end up that way because they have done something that launches them into the public eye. The "reality television" category seems to be the most vulnerable to producing the celebrities who are here for the moment and gone as soon as the next season of the reality show begins. This is true for shows like *Survivor*, *The Bachelor*, and similar formats where the person of the day goes through all the hoops and challenges of the program, wins or does not win, and then fades back into obscurity.

However, there is a big difference between the reality television star and the Internet micro-celebrity. Those who use the Internet for exposure are not always doing it just for the pursuit of well-knownness. Take the example of Peter Hollens, a YouTube micro-celebrity who is using that format to promote his musical career. He has patrons whose donations make it possible for him to pursue being a musician on a more or less full-time basis. It could be argued that the love of something like music is as big a motivator for micro-celebrity as is the desire for fame. For musicians who are not prominent enough to have a recording contract, the Internet has provided this venue to pursue music as a full-time venture without having to have the contract that would have been required a generation ago.

## TRADITIONAL CELEBRITIES USE TWITTER AND OTHER SOCIAL MEDIA

Marwick and boyd (2011) argue that what they call "networked media" has changed the face of celebrity in a fundamental way. One of the biggest changes is that celebrities can take the matter of publicity into their own hands and no longer have to use publicists as a "go between." Direct communication with the public has become a prominent way for celebrities to connect with audiences. Their examples are Mariah Carey, Miley Cyrus, and Perez Hilton, celebrity

Tweeters who use the medium in order to connect with fans, "perform" relationships with other stars, or simply Tweet about other stars, as in the case of Hilton who is a noteworthy paparazzi and online gossip columnist.

Online gossip on social media is similar in kind to what was going on in the 1930s with Walter Winchell's newspaper and radio gossip columns. The difference today is that during Winchell's time, if you wanted to question or reply to something in the column, you had to find another column to print your response or you had to approach the intimidating Winchell and ask for a retraction, something that wasn't at all easy to do. Today a gossipy Tweet can be answered by a responding Tweet, which can effectively shut down the gossip or might just escalate it. The Twitter dynamic is complex, and Twitter wars among both celebrities and fans abound.

## A CASE EXAMPLE

When looking at 21st-century de-massified media, Josh Groban provides an example of a new model for celebrity careers. Groban was still recording his first CD as a pop music star when he was asked to appear on an episode of *Ally McBeal* (2001). Playing a character who sings at the end of the episode, the viewer reaction was explosive. The network was overwhelmed with calls the next morning asking, "Who was that young man?" and "Was that really him singing?" as his big voice didn't really fit with his slight build and youthful appearance. What Groban did next was reflective of the "new order" of media; he opened a website for himself, created a chat board on it, and proceeded to chat online with the 100 or so self-identified new fans of a career still in its infancy.

Because he had signed a recording contract with Warner Brothers, he still began his career with a manager and agents, and they were very invested in "managing" his image. Various interviews have explored the ways that a mainstream "boy next door" image was cultivated for this then very young singer who was singing classically styled pop music. The next defining moment of his career, when things really took off, was a segment on news program 20/20 on April 12, 2002. The program tied together all the places where Groban had appeared thus far including singing the National Anthem for the World Series, singing at the closing ceremonies of the 2002 Winter Olympics, and appearing on *Ally McBeal*. The next week after that program aired, Groban's debut album went from 112 on the Billboard album chart to the top 10. He has never looked back since. The key piece that a television news program played in Groban's success cannot be underestimated. Mass media can still be a player in careers, even in an era of de-massified media.

Around 2008, Groban, by then 27 years old, broke ties with his former managers, hired new representation, and cultivated in earnest a newer image that was less managed and more connected to his fan base. His appearances in various Jimmy Kimmel episodes and pranks marked a shift to a newer image and different kind of more "adult" and risqué humor. He also began appearing in programs like *Never Mind the Buzzcocks*, a British television series that featured celebrities in competing teams and included irreverent humor, often at the expense of the celebrity. Groban's first appearance on this show was in December of 2008, and in 2010, he was invited back to host.

In the spirit of this career redirection, Groban made his first Tweet in July of 2009 and began the ensuing long conversation with both his fans and the general public, including the world of other celebrities. Through Twitter, Groban has networked in order to meet other celebrities as well as to talk to his fans. He is considered an influential celebrity Twitter user. He has actually even connected with television work on Twitter, a notable example being when Mindy Kaling of *The Office* direct-tweeted him in 2011 to ask him if he wanted to appear on the show, an example of how social media is even circumventing the traditional channels of agents and managers to help performers get work.

After a series of ridiculous Tweets in September 2013, where Groban pretended to accidentally Tweet instead of text about "hiding a body," one of his classic Twitter pranks, Buzzfeed (www.buzzfeed. com), a celebrity gossip website, had this to say:

> In a brief, albeit weird, look into the life of a celebrity or a constructed sketch designed to engaged, intrigue, and get a few laughs? Either way it shows the power – and possibilities – of celebrity Twitter accounts. While many celebs use social media to push their products or communicate with fans, it seems that The Grobster has realized the ridiculousness of the frenzy of celebrity worship and has used it to his advantage – and our entertainment.
>
> If you're not following @JoshGroban then you should. He's been listed on the Top Twitter Feeds To Follow for two years in a row.

In addition, one of the high points of Groban's Twitter career has been the two occasions when he went on the Jimmy Kimmel show to create songs from Tweets, first those of Kanye West and later those of Donald Trump. Groban is an example of how, by not taking Twitter terribly seriously, he has used it to draw in a new audience of fans who may not care for his music but appreciate his style of humor. Groban has also not backed off from using Twitter for a political platform, candidly expressing (as do many celebrities) his political opinions.

One of the hallmarks of Groban's Twitter behavior is his frequent Tweets to fans and his frequent favoriting of fans' Tweets. Marwick and boyd (2011) describe different ways celebrities choose to use Twitter, and Groban definitely falls in the more interactive way, using Twitter to create connections with fans. A piece I wrote about celebrities as "friendly acquaintances" (Stever, 2016a) recounted situations where Groban met fans in person, known to him on Twitter, and greeted those fans by their Twitter handles. Additionally, my students and I looked at numerous celebrity Twitter pages and determined that this interactive style was quite common for the celebrities studied.

These included Nathan Fillian, William Sadler, Jeri Ryan, Brent Spiner, William Shatner, and others, all celebrities we had determined were tweeting their own accounts (a fact we knew mostly through self-report from the celebrity at things like science fiction conventions or in media interviews).

## OTHER EXAMPLES

Click, Hyunji, and Willson Holladay (2013) found that Lady Gaga had made a similar use of social media in order to engage with her fans, or her "Little Monsters," as she calls them. The fans have embraced her term for them and used it as a form of self-identification, with Twitter handles like @gagamonster96, and @gagamonster13, etc. (there are dozens of these). In addition, others self-identify as fans with Twitter names like @gagaloverNE, @KingLadyGaga, and @ladygaga8596.

Consistent with the notion of social media as a "performance" as described by Marwick and boyd (2011), Gaga has said, "My whole life is a performance . . . I have to up the ante every day" (Stein & Michelson, 2009 p. 109). She has huge followings on Facebook (56 million as of March 7, 2018), Twitter (77.5 million as of March 7, 2018), and YouTube (1.2 billion views). With this fan/celebrity relationship in particular, the relationship is not imaginary (Caughey, 1984) but rather is reciprocated on Twitter by "Mother Monster" who actually follows 128,000 Twitter accounts, many of whom are fans.

In 2015, Sofia Katsali published the piece "How to Use Social Media if You Are a Celebrity." The article included three rules: (1) Don't be boring; (2) Engage Engage Engage; and (3) Make your fans feel special. Her advice included this set of examples:

> Reblog posts from your fans in Tumblr, like Taylor Swift. Answer fan questions on Periscope like Jose Bautista. And don't forget the little things; Reply to a few tweets every week. "Like" a couple of comments below your Facebook posts. Send some love to your

talented fans who drew a picture of you and uploaded it on Instagram.

This, in fact, appears to be the way many celebrities are now interacting on social media with a resulting boost to their follower numbers and overall careers. Social media is no longer just the domain of the micro-celebrity but instead is being used by celebrities at all levels.

## INSTANT CELEBRITY

Within social media, there is a current media trend, often referred to as "going viral," where instant celebrity is afforded to someone in part because of the presence of cell phones to record everything in the moment. Thus, instant heroes are created as with James Shaw Jr., the man who took down a mass shooter at a Waffle House in April 2018. These instant celebrities can sometimes have their fame extended because of movements born of their experience as when the Parkland, Florida, school shooting victims in February, 2018, started a campaign for gun control after that mass shooting. Thus, Anthony Borges, Emma Gonzales, and David Hogg are among students who gained international renown for their part in mobilizing this movement and were featured on the cover of *Time* magazine, April 2, 2018.

## WHEN IT BACKFIRES

Social media can be a double-edged sword for those using it to promote both career and a connection to a fan base. Being honest about political views or expressing thoughts that reflect racism, sexism, or other biases can be detrimental to a celebrity's career. Whether Tweeting about support for a political candidate or being candid about one's beliefs about a minority group, the risk is that those of your fan base who don't agree with you might decide to no longer be a fan. In addition, for those celebrities who have been caught using social media for inappropriate kinds of posts or statements, it can be a career ender. Examples might include Anthony Weiner's accidental Tweet of a racy photo in 2011, causing him to resign from his United States congressional seat, or Charlie Sheen losing his role on *Two and a Half Men* after a Twitter rant against his boss, also in 2011. In addition, instant celebrities like those mentioned above can become the targets of social media harassment for expressing controversial views. This is the dark side of social media and has to be weighed against any benefits that this media format might provide.

# EPILOGUE

What can we conclude about celebrity today in the 21st century? Some views on the topic are cynical, seeing celebrity as only a means for pursuing profit and riches. "Rich and famous" is how the saying goes. Is there another way to view celebrity beyond that stereotype?

In 1990, I spent a significant amount of time with the fans of Paul McCartney. I attended two Beatlefests and spent time at local fan gatherings with a small group of fans in Phoenix, Arizona (where I lived at the time). It was clear to me from the time I spent with this group of mostly women that they had a deep respect and affection for Sir Paul McCartney, and while I had been a Beatle fan as a child, it was equally clear that I was not "one of them." They told me so. They were kind when they said it, simply pointing out that having been a childhood fan of The Beatles was not the same as their longer commitment to the career of this specific Beatle. I had to agree. McCartney was touring that year, and I attended his show in Phoenix where I collected survey data and interviewed fans. He is one of the great superstars of our time. The Beatles have that iconic status that was discussed in an earlier chapter of this book. In a century of media stars, they stand out among the biggest.

On March 24, 2018, as a reaction to the school shooting in Parkland, Florida, where 17 people were killed, marches were held across the United States to protest gun violence. Millions turned out for these marches. In New York City, Sir Paul McCartney was among the crowd, wearing a t-shirt that said "We Can End Gun Violence," where he said to a reporter, "I'm like everyone. One of my best friends was killed by gun violence right around here, so it's important to me not just to march today but to take action tomorrow." I posted his photo and the report on my Facebook page when I found it, and of all the stories of that day, this one got the most likes and shares of anything I posted. People were moved by the presence of McCartney during the march.

In psychology we study things like motivation and emotion, and also meaningfulness. Memories are most vivid when there is specific meaning for them, and one of the strongest motivators of human behavior is an association with long-term and deep emotion. A celebrity like Sir Paul McCartney marching against gun violence in memory of his fallen friend, John Lennon, has a meaningfulness that stirs our emotions and inspires our respect. The death of Lennon at the hands of a mentally ill fan, shot down in the prime of his life, represents much that was bad and difficult about the life of a celebrity in the 20th century, and McCartney marching in his memory represents much that is good about celebrity influence in the 21st century. His message on a cell phone interview with activist Lorna Mae Johnson to young people was "Get out and vote. Make things change. It's up to you." Because of who he is and what he was marching for, he had our attention and more people listened to him.

Celebrity can be a way to market a brand. It can also be a way to magnify an important message. It is important to consider both when we consider the influence of celebrity. Celebrities are each unique individuals. Some of them, people of integrity like Sir Paul, brave enough to march with the masses, speak to the public in a unique voice magnified by the attention that celebrity commands in today's world.

# FURTHER READING

Bandura, A. (2001). Social cognitive theory of mass communication. *Media Psychology*, 3(3), 265–299.

Albert Bandura was an important mid-20th-century psychologist who played a key role in expanding the traditional behaviorist approaches. This article applies his theory specifically to the domain of mass media.

Bennett, J. (2011). *Television personalities: Stardom and the small screen*. New York: Routledge.

Bennett does a great job differentiating television celebrity from other forms including the theory behind these differences.

Cashmore, E. (2014). *Celebrity culture*. New York: Routledge.

This book has a more extended discussion of many of the topics covered here and features an extensive timeline of events related to the history of celebrity in the appendix.

Giles, D. C. (2018). *Twenty-first century: Fame in digital culture*. Bingley, Yorks: Emerald.

Some topics that are outside the scope of this book are covered in Giles' recent book, including the implications of celebrity as an integral part of the political process, and how social media in particular has been influential (see Chapter 10).

Hazan, C., & Shaver, P. (1994). Attachment as an organizational framework for research on close relationship. *Psychological Inquiry*, 5, 1–22.

This article explains the way that these researches have extended the attachment concept developed by Bowlby and Ainsworth to apply it to adult relationships.

Levinson, D. J. (1986). A conception of adult development. *American Psychologist*, 41(1), 3.

A concise description of Levinson's theory of adult development.

McLeod, S. A. (2007). Bowlby's attachment theory. *Simply Psychology*. Retrieved from www.simplypsychology.org/bowlby.html

This article explains basic aspects of attachment theory.

McLeod, S. A. (2008). Social identity theory. *Simply Psychology*. Retrieved from www.simplypsychology.org/social-identity-theory.html

An article on the basics of Tajfel's theory.

McLeod, S. A. (2015). *Skinner – operant conditioning*. Retrieved from www.simplypsychology.org/operant-conditioning.html

Basics of behaviorism are covered in this article.

McLeod, S. A. (2017). Erik Erikson. *Simply Psychology*. Retrieved from www.simplypsychology.org/Erik-Erikson.html

This website gives the basics of Erikson's lifespan theory of development with descriptions of each of his stages.

Sannicolas, N. (1997). Erving Goffman, dramaturgy, and on-line relationships. *Cibersociology Site*. Retrieved from www.cybersociology.com/files/1_2_sannicolas.html

A discussion relating Goffman's theories to online relationships.

Stever, G. S. (2013). Mediated vs. parasocial relationships: An attachment perspective. *Journal of Media Psychology*, 17(3), 1–31.

The application of attachment theory to parasocial relationships is explained in this article.

# REFERENCES

Abidin, C. (2015). Communicative intimacies: Influencers and perceived inter-connectedness. *Ada: A Journal of Gender, New Media, and Technology*, (8). Retrieved from http://adanewmedia.org/blog/2015/11/01/issue8-abidin/

Abidin, C. (2017). Influencer extravaganza. In L. Hjorth, H. Horst, G. Bell, & A. Galloway (Eds.), The Routledge companion to digital ethnography (pp. 158–168). New York: Routledge.

Barry, E. (2008). Celebrity, cultural production and public life. *International Journal of Cultural Studies*, 11, 251–258. doi:10.1177/1367877908092583

Basil, M. D. (1996). Identification as a mediator of celebrity effects. *Journal of Broadcasting & Electronic Media*, 40(4), 478–495.

Baumeister, R. F., & Leary, M. R. (1995). The need to belong: Desire for interpersonal attachments as a fundamental human motivation. *Psychological Bulletin*, 117(3), 497.

Bloland, S. E. (2005). *In the shadow of fame: A memoir by the daughter of Erik H. Erikson*. New York: Viking.

Boorstin, D. J. (1961). *The image: A guide to pseudo-events in America*. New York: Vintage Books.

Boykoff, M. T., & Goodman, M. K. (2009). Conspicuous redemption? Reflections on the promises and perils of the 'celebritization' of climate change. *Geoforum*, 40(3), 395–406.

Braudy, L. (1997). *The frenzy of renown: Fame & its history*. New York: Vintage Books.

Brock, C. (2006). *The feminization of fame 1750–1830*. London: Palgrave MacMillan.

Caughey, J. L. (1984). *Imaginary social worlds: A cultural approach*. Lincoln: University of Nebraska Press.

Chernow, R. (2005). *Alexander Hamilton*. New York: Penguin.

Click, M. A., Hyunji, L., & Willson Holladay, H. (2013). Making monsters: Lady Gaga, fan identification, and social media. *Popular Music and Society, 36*(3), 360–379. doi:10.1080/03007766.2013.798546

Couldry, N. (2003). *Media rituals: A critical approach*. London: Psychology Press.

Couldry, N. (2004). Theorising media as practice. *Social Semiotics, 14*(2), 115–132.

Driessens, O. (2013). The celebritization of society and culture: Understanding the structural dynamics of celebrity culture. *International Journal of Cultural Studies, 16*(6), 641–657.

Driessens, O. (2015). Expanding celebrity studies' research agenda: Theoretical opportunities and methodological challenges in interviewing celebrities. *Celebrity Studies, 6*(2), 192–205.

Dumenco, S. (2016). Yes he can? Here's how Trump could win | Campaign trail. *AdAge*. Retrieved September 24, 2016, from http://adage.com/article/campaign-trail/trump-win/305800/

Dyer, R. (2004). *Heavenly bodies: Film stars and society*. New York: Psychology Press.

Ferris, K. O., & Harris, S. R. (2011). *Stargazing: Celebrity, fame, and social interaction*. London: Routledge.

Fraser, B. P., & Brown, W. J. (2002). Media, celebrities, and social influence: Identification with Elvis Presley. *Mass Communication & Society, 5*(2), 183–206.

Friedman, D. M. (2014). *Wilde in America: Oscar Wilde and the invention of modern celebrity*. New York & London: W.W. Norton & Company.

Gabler, N. (1995). *Winchell: Gossip, power and the culture of celebrity*. New York: Vintage Books.

Gamson, J. (1994). *Claims to fame: Celebrity in contemporary America*. Berkeley, CA: University of California Press.

Gardner, A. (1990). *Ava: My story*. New York: Bantam & Greenwood Press.

Garland, R. (2010). Celebrity ancient and modern. *Society, 47*(6), 484–488.

Giles, D. (2000). *Illusions of immortality: A psychology of fame and celebrity*. Basingstoke: Palgrave Macmillan.

Gledhill, C. (Ed.). (1991). *Stardom: Industry of desire*. New York: Psychology Press.

Glueck, G. (1980). Retrieved from www.nytimes.com/1980/04/08/archives/salk-studies-mans-future-salk-studies-mans-future-renewed-interest.html?sq=Salk+Studies+Man%2527s+Future&scp=1&st=p

Goffman, E. (1959). *The presentation of self in everyday life*. New York: Anchor Books.

Greenberg, J., Kosloff, S., Solomon, S., Cohen, F., & Landau, M. (2010). Toward understanding the fame game: The effect of mortality salience on the appeal of fame. *Self and Identity, 9*(1), 1–18.

Greenwood, D. N. (2013). Fame, Facebook, and Twitter: How attitudes about fame predict frequency and nature of social media use. *Psychology of Popular Media Culture, 2*(4), 222.

Greenwood, D. N., Long, C. R., & Dal Cin, S. (2013). Fame and the social self: The need to belong, narcissism, and relatedness predict the appeal of fame. *Personality and Individual Differences, 55*(5), 490–495.

Harrington, C. (2010). *Soap fans: Pursuing pleasure and making meaning in everyday life*. Philadelphia: Temple University Press.

Hills, M. (2016). From para-social to multisocial interaction. In P. D. Marshall & S. Redmond (Eds.), *A companion to celebrity* (pp. 463–482). Malden, MA: Wiley-Blackwell.

Holmes, S., & Redmond, S. (Eds.). (2006). *Framing celebrity: New directions in celebrity culture*. London: Routledge.

Holmes, S., & Redmond, S. (Eds.) (2012). *Framing celebrity: New directions in celebrity culture*. London: Routledge.

Horton, D., & Richard Wohl, R. (1956). Mass communication and para-social interaction: Observations on intimacy at a distance. *Psychiatry, 19*(3), 215–229.

Inglis, F. (2010). *A short history of celebrity*. Princeton, NJ: Princeton University Press.

Jenson, J. (1992). Fandom as pathology: The consequences of characterization. In *The adoring audience: Fan culture and popular media* (pp. 9–29). London: Routledge.

Katsali, S. (2015). *How to use social media if you are a celebrity*. Retrieved from www.huffingtonpost.com/sofia-katsali/how-to-use-social-media-i_b_8752130.html

Kennedy, A. (2016). *Einstein: A life of genius* (The true story of Albert Einstein) (Historical Biographies of Famous People). New York: Fritzen Publishing LLC

Kohut, A., Keeter, S., Doherty, C., Dimock, M., Funk, C., Wike, R., . . . Albrittain, J. (2006). *How young people view their lives, futures and politics: A portrait of "Generation Next"*. Washington, DC: The Pew Research Center.

Kurzman, C., Anderson, C., Key, C., Lee, Y. O., Moloney, M., Silver, A., & Van Ryn, M. W. (2007). Celebrity status. *Sociological Theory, 25*(4), 347–367.

Lamare, A. (2014). Retrieved from www.celebritynetworth.com/articles/entertainment-articles/amazing-story-keanu-reeves-gave-away-75-million-matrix-salary/

Luckhurst, M., & Moody, J. (Eds.). (2005). *Theatre and celebrity in Britain, 1660–2000* (p. 173). Basingstoke: Palgrave Macmillan.

Maltby, J., Day, L., Giles, D., Gillett, R., Quick, M., Langcaster-James, H., & Linley, P.A. (2008). Implicit theories of a desire for fame. *British Journal of Psychology, 99*(2), 279–292.

Mander, J. (1978). *Four arguments for the elimination of television* (pp. 15–16). New York: Quill.

Marshall, P. D. (1997). *Celebrity and power: Fame in contemporary culture.* Minneapolis, MN: University of Minnesota Press.

Marwick, A. E., & boyd, D. (2011). I tweet honestly, I tweet passionately: Twitter users, context collapse, and the imagined audience. *New Media & Society, 13*(1), 114–133.

McCarley, N. G., & Escoto, C. A. (2003). Celebrity worship and psychological type. *North American Journal of Psychology, 5*(1), 117–120.

McCracken, G. (1989). Who is the celebrity endorser? Cultural foundations of the endorsement process. *Journal of Consumer Research, 16*(3), 310–321.

McCullough, D. (2002). *John Adams.* New York: Simon and Schuster.

McCullough, D. (2015). *The Wright Brothers.* New York: Simon and Schuster.

McCutcheon, L. E., Maltby, J., Houran, J., & Ashe, D. D. (2004). *Celebrity worshippers: Inside the minds of stargazers.* Baltimore, MD: PublishAmerica.

Miller, A. (2013). *Timebends: A life.* New York: Grove & Atlantic, Inc.

Mills, C. W. (1981). *The power elite* [1956]. London: Oxford University Press.

Mole, T. (2009). *Romanticism and celebrity culture, 1750–1850* (T. Mole, Ed.). Cambridge: Cambridge University Press.

Myers, I., & Myers, P. (2010). *Gifts differing: Understanding personality type.* London: Nicholas Brealey Publishing.

Park, R. E. (1950). *Race and culture.* New York: Free Press.

Parry-Giles, T. (2008). Fame, celebrity, and the legacy of John Adams. *Western Journal of Communication, 72*(1), 83–101.

Pinker, S. (2015). *The village effect: How face-to-face contact can make us healthier and happier.* Toronto, Canada: Vintage Books.

Postman, N. (2006). *Amusing ourselves to death: Public discourse in the age of show business.* New York: Penguin.

Putnam, R. D. (2001). *Bowling alone: The collapse and revival of American community.* New York: Simon and Schuster.

Robinson, A. (2015). *Stepping into the light: Sources of an actor's craft.* Los Angeles, CA: Figueroa Press.

Rojek, C. (2001). *Celebrity.* New York: John Wiley & Sons, Ltd.

Schickel, R. (2000). *Intimate strangers: The culture of celebrity in America.* Chicago: Ivan R. Dee.

Schwartz, S. H. (2012). An overview of the Schwartz theory of basic values. *Online Readings in Psychology and Culture, 2*(1). Retrieved from https://doi.org/10.9707/2307-0919.1116

Senft, T. M. (2008). *Camgirls: Celebrity and community in the age of social networks.* New York: Peter Lang.

Soukup, C. (2006). Hitching a ride on a star: Celebrity, fandom, and identification on the World Wide Web. *Southern Communication Journal, 71*(4), 319–337.

Stein, J. D., & Michelson, N. (2009). The lady is a vamp. *Out, Out Mag.*

Sternheimer, K. (2015). *Celebrity culture and the American dream: Stardom and social mobility.* New York: Routledge.

Stever, G. (1991a). The celebrity appeal questionnaire. *Psychological Reports, 68,* 859–866.

Stever, G. (1991b). Imaginary social relationships and personality correlates. *Journal of Psychological Type, 21,* 68–76.

Stever, G. (1994). *Parasocial attachments: Motivational antecedents* (Doctoral Dissertation), Arizona State University, Tempe, AZ.

Stever, G. (1995). Gender by type interaction effects in mass media subcultures. *Journal of Psychological Type, 32,* 3–12.

Stever, G. (2008). The celebrity appeal questionnaire: Sex, entertainment or leadership. *Psychological Reports, 103,* 113–120.

Stever, G. (2009). Parasocial and social interaction with celebrities: Classification of media fans. *Journal of Media Psychology, 14*(3), 1–39.

Stever, G. (2011a). 1989 vs. 2009: A comparative analysis of music superstars Michael Jackson and Josh Groban, and their fans. *Journal of Media Psychology, 16*(1).

Stever, G. (2011b). Celebrity worship: Critiquing a construct. *Journal of Applied Social Psychology, 41*(6).

Stever, G. S. (2011c). Fan behavior and lifespan development theory: Explaining para-social and social attachment to celebrities. *Journal of Adult Development, 18*(1), 1–7.

Stever, G. (2016a). Meeting Josh Groban (again): Fan/celebrity contact as ordinary behavior. *International Association for the Study of Popular Music Journal*, 6(1), 104–120.

Stever, G. (2016b). Parasocial interaction: Concept and impact (incl. measurement and scales). In *International encyclopedia of media effects*. London: Wiley-Blackwell.

Stever, G., & Lawson, K. (2013). Twitter as a way for celebrities to communicate with fans: Implications for the study of parasocial interaction. *North American Journal of Psychology*, 15(2), 597–612.

Swain, M. H. (1982). Abigail Adams: An American woman. *The History Teacher*, 15(2), 292.

Tajfel, H. (1970). Experiments in intergroup discrimination. *Scientific American*, 223(5), 96–103.

Thomson, M. (2006). Human brands: Investigating antecedents to consumers' strong attachments to celebrities. *Journal of Marketing*, 70(3), 104–119.

Toffler, A. (1980). *The third wave* (Vol. 484). New York: Bantam Books.

Toffler, A. (1990). *Powershift: Knowledge, wealth, and violence at the edge of the 21st century*. New York: Bantam.

Turner, G. (2004). *Understanding celebrity*. Thousand Oaks: Sage Publication.

Turner, G. (2010). Approaching celebrity studies. *Celebrity Studies*, 1(1), 11–20.

Turner, G. (2014). *Understanding celebrity*. Thousand Oaks: Sage Publication.

Van de Rijt, A., Shor, E., Ward, C., & Skiena, S. (2013). Only 15 minutes? The social stratification of fame in printed media. *American Sociological Review*, 78(2), 266–289.

Van Krieken, R. (2012). *Celebrity society*. London: Routledge.

Wolf, N. (2013). *The beauty myth: How images of beauty are used against women*. New York: Random House.

Yahr, E., Moore, C., & Chow, E. (2015). *How we went from 'Survivor' to more than 300 reality shows: A complete guide*. Retrieved from www.washingtonpost.com/graphics/entertainment/reality-tv-shows/

Yousafzai, M. (2013). *I am Malala: The girl who stood up for education and was shot by the Taliban*. London: Hachette.